DEAR BOBBY
A PORTRAIT OF DEPRESSION, ADDICTION, LOSS AND LOVE

JACKIE YOUNG

Printed in the United States of America
ISBN: 978-1-956019-29-2 (paperback)
ISBN: 978-1-956019-30-8 (ebook)

Canoe Tree Press

4697 Main Street
Manchester Center, VT 05255
Canoe Tree Press is a division of DartFrog Books

Cover photo taken at The Freed Theater in Chester, PA
Photo credit: Nick Marciano

Grateful acknowledgment is made for permission to reproduce the following material:

"Rescue" by Lauren Daigle/Jason Ingram/Paul Mabury
Copyright © 2018 CentricSongs (SESAC) See You At The Pub (SESAC). Administered at CapitolCMGPublishing.com. All rights reserved. Used by permission.
So Essential Tunes (SESAC) / Fellow Ships Music (SESAC) /
ICM Crescendo Royalty Publishing (SESAC). Administered at EssentialMusicPublishing.com. All rights reserved. Used by permission.

Saving a Life © 2008 by Charles Morris and Janet Morris. Used by permission of David C. Cook. May not be further reproduced. All rights reserved.

Healing for Damaged Emotions © 1981, 2015 by David A. Seamands. Used by permission of David C Cook. May not be further reproduced. All rights reserved.

To Bob – Thank you for letting me rely on your strength when I had none of my own and for your patience. But most of all, thank you for doing something that I wasn't sure was possible and that's making me laugh again. I love you.

To Hannah – I bought a dress for you in Hong Kong before I realized I was pregnant with you. I knew that one day I was going to have a girl, that your name would be Hannah Yael and that I already loved you. What I didn't know was how much I was going to need you. You have always been a joy and have grown into both a joy and a friend. I love you.

To Bobby – Thank you for writing this with me. Thank you for leaving us your poems and journals. Thank you for sharing so much of yourself through your writing. I know for certain that I wouldn't have finished this without you. I love you.

ACKNOWLEDGMENTS

There are several different directions I could go with this because I have been blessed with wonderful family and friends. The short list:

To my parents, Harry and Jackie Burress, and sisters, Lil Thompson, Eileen Shelton and Loretta Marmer - I love you and thank you for always being there for me and for all the beautiful people you've brought into my life, from Willy to Maeve.

Thank you to the Young Family for your encouragement.

MaryEllen Healy - When I left you a message about Bobby's death, you didn't call me back; you dropped what you were doing and came over. It's one of the rare times we ran out of things to say, but you spoke volumes by your presence. I treasure our friendship.

Fran and Carol Krawiec – You both make the world a more compassionate, more hospitable and more loving place. We've been on the receiving end of your kindness so many times and I know we have a lot of company. It's priceless to have friends who understand what we're going through and continually love, support, and pray for us. Thank you for sharing your beach house and dolphin watching with us. Even if you do make up the dolphin watching rules as you go along. Looking at you Fran.

Many thanks to Bobby's friends. So many of you are our friends too and have helped to carry us through the past three years, just as you helped to carry Bobby through his difficult times. We welcomed every message and card you sent. We're grateful for all the times you checked on us and that you remember Bobby on his birthday. So many of you weren't just friends to Bobby, you were lifelines. To everyone who picked him up for meetings, offered help and provided encouragement, thank you. I began to write a short list of names, but there is no short list. There was always one more person I could add. We know who you are;

you know who you are; Bobby knows who you are. Thank you to all of you from the bottom of our hearts.

Just as there is no short list for Bobby's friends, there is no short list for everyone who has cared for us since we lost Bobby. Thank you to those of you who have prayed, visited, texted, called and sent cards. To the artists and poets who shared your creativity with us, thank you. To those of you who cooked for us and those who left boxes of food on our doorstep, thank you. For trees planted in Bobby's memory, thank you. Every one of you is a blessing.

When planning Bobby's Memorial Service, I got to the point where I couldn't make one more decision. Nancy Blackburn, without you, there would have been no music. Dottie and Matty Rysak, without you, there would have been no food. Woodlyn Baptist, without you, there would have been no church. Thank you all.

Thank you to my proofreaders, Bob Young, Judith Bonaduce and Carol Krawiec for your support, encouragement and helpful suggestions.

Many thanks to my editors, Eileen Shelton and Hannah Young. I don't think either of you realize how much you've improved this. As Captain Jack Sparrow said in Pirates of the Caribbean, "I think we've all arrived at a very special place. Spiritually, ecumenically, grammatically." Thank you for all you've done grammatically, but even more for taking a disjointed collection of quotes, poems, letters and thoughts and pushing it all into book form. You were right about chapters. I was wrong.

To Bobby, Dan, Ben and Tim – Could never be heaven without you.[1]

---

[1] "Brand New - Could never Be Heaven," Genius, accessed November 5, 2021, https://genius.com/Brand-new-could-never-be-heaven-lyrics.

PREFACE

Anyone who has been impacted by depression and addiction knows how difficult, and often devastating, this combination can be. Our son, Bobby, died at the age of 29 from a drug overdose. He had a depressive personality and battled a heroin addiction for 10 years. When someone so young dies from something that seems preventable, they are often defined by their deaths. However, our lives are really defined by the dash in between the birth and death dates on our tombstones.[2] We don't control the dates, but to an extent, we can control the dash. Sadly, for those of us who have lost a child to addiction, we have to come to grips with a son or daughter who lost control of their dash.

Following a child's death from addiction, families and friends will often either join existing organizations or will establish foundations to raise awareness and support in their child's memory. This is our attempt to add to the conversation. We read social media posts written by parents we've never met who have also lost a child to an overdose. Whether their death was the result of a relapse, experimentation, or a long slow decline, we can identify with the sense of intense pain and loss in each post. We know how helpful it is to be able to relate to other people in similar circumstances. I'll always remember reading that another mom was afraid of the phone because the call might be bad news. I was relieved to know there was at least one other person out there who braced herself when the phone rang.

We loved Bobby every minute of every day. But we frequently didn't know what to do to help him. Addiction is brutal. It kept knocking us down, and every time we came back up, we were in unfamiliar territory. Not everything we did was right. Not everything we did was wrong. We did the best we

---

[2] Linda M. Ellis, *Live Your Dash: Make Every Moment Matter* (New York: Sterling Ethos, 2014).

knew how to do at the time. If you're reading this and have struggled, or are still struggling, with someone you love who is battling an addiction, I hope that by sharing our story it will bring a degree of comfort to know that there are others who understand how difficult it is. I'm not writing this because I think our story is special. I'm writing it because I know it's not. I realize this runs counter to the reasons people usually write memoirs. However, those of us who love someone who has struggled with addiction are used to a world that runs counter: to hopes, to dreams, to what we want, to what we expect, to what we pray for.

Bobby is also adding to the conversation through some of his journal entries and poetry, which are included here. He was an intense individual, which, coupled with depression and addiction, proved exhausting. When he chose to go to Kensington, a neighborhood in Philadelphia known for drug use, to play Russian roulette with his life one more time, he was physically and emotionally depleted.

That said, we believe what he wrote can provide a sense of empathy, understanding and even encouragement to those who are still struggling, for those who "think the same thoughts and sense the same feelings and each perfectly understands the other."[3] One of his friends, Eric, told us that Bobby's death saved his life and that Bobby is a "huge driving force" for him. By living a meaningful life, Eric hopes to make the friends he's lost to addiction proud and to help give meaning to their deaths. If you're fighting addiction, we hope you realize how significant you are and that you also find purpose, lasting recovery and hope for your future.

What follows was written at different times by different people, but primarily by Bobby and me. *Plain Songs, Siren Songs* and *Redemption Songs* refer to the names Bobby gave to his poetry collections.

---

[3] Lin Yutang, *The Importance of Living* (New York: Reynal & Hitchcock, 1937), ix.

Eric and Bobby at the Eagles Superbowl Parade, 2.8.18

CHAPTER ONE

How It Ends

Yeah, you already know how this will end.[4]

⟺

I am ready for Heaven
I sit at the gates
Pleading Peter let me in

I died today, or maybe yesterday. I can't remember or say exactly, for does it really matter. Time is irrelevant to me now, being dead. I now have transcended time, and see things in an infinite purity, hidden from us in our earthly bodies...There is...nothing humans have all conjured up in their mystical minds. There is simply spirit. I am still coming to grips with leaving the earthly realm. It was not on the best terms. Not a suicide, but my final overdose. I left a path of destruction and hurt many people. I'm not sure what to do now. I'm currently floating above my parents. As they weep, I weep. I cannot believe I have done this to them. Emotions, unfortunately, do not dissipate.... I will be hating to inform you of many things, answers, and answers which just lead to a plethora of new questions. Answers are tricky like that; they are so frequently unsatisfying. I had so many questions in life. So many questions I was tortured. And now, being dead, I hope to find some answers. I'll go looking for Jesus tomorrow, but today I am with my parents, holding them as their world is turning

---

[4] Devotchka, *How It Ends*, Genius, accessed September 1, 2020, https://genius.com/Devotchka-how-it-ends-lyrics.

DEAR BOBBY

upside down. They were prepared for this moment as best they could. Yet nothing can truly prepare you for the death of your first-born boy. "My beautiful boy" my father would call me. I was truly loved by many people. But felt none of it. Now I do. Being a sober soul, I feel everything. I am going to continue to comfort my parents as we cry. I'll talk to you guys later.

— Bobby, undated journal entry

⟺

Dear Bobby,

It's been 41 days since we last saw you, 38 days since our last contact, 37 days since you left us, and 36 days since we got the phone call from the investigator at the Philadelphia Medical Examiner's Office. We knew that you were tired and ready to go. You told us as much. We, however, were still hopeful and would never have been ready to let you go. When we got the news, Dad and I waited almost a day before we told anyone. Maybe we thought letting other people know would make it too real. Daddy talked to the examiner on Saturday night, and then we told Hannah Sunday morning. We were able to positively ID you over the phone by your tattoos. As you know, I've never been a big fan of them, even though you had some pretty cool ones, but I was grateful for them that night. A drive into Philadelphia to positively identify you would have been a nightmare. Sunday evening, we started calling and people started coming over. Grammy, Aunt Peaches and Uncle Bill, Neese, Uncle Larry and Aunt Loretta, Jules, Grace, MaryEllen, Fran and Carol, Ben, Tim, Rossi, Josiah. Ferry was in Ireland, as you knew.

On Monday night, Ben got a bunch of your friends together at Milk Boy in Philly and The Dead Milkmen played. I didn't realize just how fitting that was until I was going through one of

14

your journals and read, "When I die, have a big party, a memorial rock concert...I want Dead Milkmen to come sing about punk rock girls." Afterwards Ben wrote to you on your Facebook page, "Tonight was perfect. We have so many amazing friends with such beautiful souls. I felt you in that room tonight. I miss you with every piece of my broken heart. I'll see you again in paradise, my beautiful and unique brother/best friend."

Your Memorial Service was Thursday night at Woodlyn Baptist Church. At times, the line was out the door and down the steps. Aunt Neese, your "#1 Ridley Mom", spoke and was incredible. You would have been so proud of her. I asked Ferry if he wanted to write a few words for the program and what he ended up writing was your eulogy. It was heartfelt, heartbreaking and funny. Perfect. Hannah read it and did a beautiful job. Ben put together a video presentation to Devotchka's "How It Ends" and it was beautiful. Daddy spoke. During the week Hannah said, "You aren't going to let him do this, are you?!" She didn't think he could hold it together. Neither did I, but he worked hard on his message and did a beautiful job as well. He only went off script once (5 seconds in) and we were able to bring him right back. I know you know how amazing that is. Devon from the Freed Theater in Chester spoke on short notice with his usual combination of strength and grace. People who didn't know you said they felt as if they now did and a few said it was the best memorial service they had ever attended. As MaryEllen said, "Not that we rate funerals..." but that made me especially pleased because there was a time during your struggle when I wondered, if the day came, if I could make it through a service. So, I'm glad we did it and glad it worked out so well. We wanted to bring glory to God for your life and to honor God and you.

For the past month, I've been writing to you just like I used to do. I would often have so much to say to try to encourage you in your sobriety or to clear things up as you came and went from the house. During those times, I had so much I wanted to tell you, but was sure at least half of it would get lost in a conversation, so I would write it down. I'm still doing this.

So many people have said that you are now free of pain and in a better place. I know in my head that this is true. But all I can feel at this point is a profound sense that you're not here. I think I can now relate a bit to how you felt when you told me once that you knew you were loved but you couldn't feel it. I know you are in the hands of a loving and merciful God, but I can't get there yet through the vast emptiness here.

Love,

Mom, Dad and Hannah

Bob, me, Hannah and Bobby in front of the church where Bob and I were married in Geneva, Switzerland. This was taken thirty-five years and a day later.

Hannah, me and Bobby in Munich, Germany

Disclaimer
This will be just one more shitty love poem
to sex
to drugs
to rock n' roll.

You think you're too young to die, huh?
well, everyday my Facebook feed
fills with people who were
too young to die.
Everyday people they loved post

on their walls, memories and pictures,
writing how their hearts ache at the passing
of one too young to die.
People who the dead disliked or even hated
also post on their walls, RIP, sad to see you go,
etc. empty bullshit like "only the good die young,"
please.
I try to watch from afar, for if I get too close
I fear I am the next to go.
You think it can never happen to you, until
you wake up in a hospital bed with an IV in your
arm and a head awhirl with Narcan.[5]
But, still, it couldn't happen to me, because
it's happening to the people all around me.

I miss the rock n' roll in dirty Philly basements
that felt punk even when it was folk.
I miss doing drugs without ending up
homeless, broke, and emotionally destitute
immediately after.
I like the tenants of pop punk music.
example: I like my friends, I remember that time you were drunk and "spilled the
apple juice in the hall,"[6] I like the ideal of that one girl all the Jesse Laceys of the
world write about, most importantly, I like the thought that none of this is really my
fault...when it is.

I had a therapist, more than one, ask me
to write a breakup letter to drugs.
I could never get very far with it

---

[5] Narcan is a medication used to reverse the effects of opioids.
[6] He must have had this phrase in quotation marks because it's very similar to a lyric by Blink-182, "Adam's Song," *Enema of the State*, 1999.

for drugs dumped me a long time ago and have since moved on.
If I was honest, I would write, "Take me
back, I can handle you again and
things can go back to how they
were when we first met."
But I know this can never be,
as drugs are busy seeing other people.

Do you remember the day the lightning bugs
began to disappear?
Now, in the stead of those tiny glowing insect dots
is only the sense of a faintly felt fear,
of growing old and
losing our illusion of safety.
Bring back the insects,
bring back the
sex
drugs
and
rock n' roll.
—Siren Songs

Photo credit Greg Irvin

I think I relate to the 'no outlet' signs lined up along the roadsides of this expansive country, filled with more than one quarter of a billion people, more than I do to any of the people who live in the houses down those 'no outlet' lanes.
—Journal entry

Chapter Two

Reality Is My Problem

I'm starting to feel
That for the first time in a decade
I have a choice
Whether to live like this or not
And I'm caught up in the same
Repetitive tangle
Awake in a dream
I never remember a thing
From starting to fall
Forgive me
I don't know when I will wake up[7]

————◆————

where did you go

what did you do

where did you wake up

I went everywhere I could

I am trying to escape

can I escape

been looking for my mind since the pixies asked me to

---

[7] "Circa Survive - Awake in a Dream," Genius, accessed September 1, 2020, https://genius.com/Circa-survive-awake-in-a-dream-lyrics.

I did everything I could
to escape myself
over oceans to London
over arctic to Beijing
over prairie and rocks to Durango
traveling looking for myself in everything else
instead of letting go
can't I escape?
I go to work here there and everywhere
What can I get for you guys today
What kind of massage would you like today
Where do you want me to bring this artwork today
Where is my guard post today
can I never get away?...
In the everlasting eternity my father believes in
I awaken
I found myself
—Siren Songs

The following letter was written in anticipation of Bobby being discharged from a rehab facility. He was in his early 20s at the time.

Dear Bobby,

We love you, we miss you, and we are very much looking forward to you coming home. We thought it would be a good idea to put some things in writing because clarity is always a good thing. You are truly at a crossroad and it's time for acceptance on your part for some of the realities of life and some responsibility for cleaning up the past couple of years and moving forward into a future that you can be proud of and enjoy.

There's a big difference between happiness and avoidance of pain. Moments of true happiness come most frequently during a life that takes responsibility and makes good decisions. When a person just tries to avoid pain through drugs or drinking, they are not laying any foundation on which to build. Life becomes a cycle of hurt and avoidance. There is no foundation, no gain, no growth, and no true happiness.

This is a good time for introspection and reflection. What is negotiable for you and what is not? Do your choices support what you value? We, of course, want the best for you. We want you to live in reality, to find your passion, to have meaningful work, good times, and wonderful friends and relationships. All these things lead to fulfillment. All these things require effort. They don't just happen. You need to choose.

I've told you many times that Satan is a master of deception. The false feel good of drugs is right out of the pit of hell. Don't think about how it feels, look at what it produces. The fact that we want the best for you does not mean we will always agree with you. We all make decisions that are not in our own best interest and can't expect others to support us in them. So, be forewarned, one of those decisions on your part would be if you need to go back to rehab, you cannot come directly back home.

We love you immensely,
Mom and Dad
XXXXXXOOOOOOO

Staring at the stars
Waiting for the scars
to heal
Questioning the sky
An absence of reply
Or at least the one I can hear
Brings upon the fear
—Journal entry

◆◆◆

Shortly after Bobby died, I was given a book, *Rainbow Remedies for Life's Stormy Times*, written by a woman who had experienced extraordinary loss over the span of four years. She collected what she learned regarding how to cope under such difficult circumstances and wrote it down to help others. One suggestion she shared that appears to be simple and self-evident, but that resonated with me, is "before treating a problem, we must learn what the problem is."[8] This made me think because, for Bobby, and many like him, we are not treating just one problem, but often two or more co-occurring problems. This makes it even more critical that we learn what the problems are.

I see posts on social media by people celebrating a given number of days or months or years clean and they are happy and thriving. I celebrate with them, of course, but it's bittersweet because Bobby didn't often get to this point because, when he wasn't using, he was frequently battling depression. It was a constant concern. He did seek treatment for it, but for the most part, his attempts were superficial and the shadows always returned. Whenever we did press for more in-depth counseling, it was difficult to get him to

---

[8] Joanne K. Hill, *Rainbow Remedies for Life's Stormy Times* (South Bend, IN: Moorhill Communications, 2002), 26.

commit. Bobby thought he could manage his depression, but his dad, Bob, and I thought this kept the door open for a relapse and we were right.

I have no doubt Bobby could have related to Russell Brand, comedian and mental health/drug rehab activist, when Brand said, "Drugs and alcohol are not my problem. Reality is my problem. Drugs and alcohol are my solution."[9] This is where I question whether we fully understood what the problem was. Not that we mourn Bobby in terms of thinking we didn't try hard enough, or to advise anyone in one direction or another, but once we knew he had started to use heroin, that was our focus, not his depression. Then, as if heroin alone wasn't deadly enough, once the extremely lethal narcotic fentanyl was mixed in with it, it became even more toxic. It's hard for me to understand how something so dangerous could be seen as an answer to anything.

Often rehabs operate as dual diagnosis treatment facilities and are equipped to treat mental health as well as substance abuse disorders. Once when I asked Bobby what this meant in terms of psychiatric care, he replied that it meant spending 15 minutes with a psychiatrist and then a prescription for Gabapentin. I suspect this was overly critical, but whatever the approach, it wasn't therapeutic or compelling enough to lead to meaningful follow up or lasting change on his part. I also realize that the best therapies can be impotent in the hands of an unwilling participant.

Drug addiction can be, and is, treated successfully, but it's not simple since it's a disease that affects both the brain and behavior. I always found this to be particularly cruel regarding addiction. We need our brains on our side, fighting with us and for us. An addiction literally puts a person's brain at war with themselves. In 1983, Dr. David Sedlak theorized that addictive thinking is "a person's inability to make consistently healthy decisions in his or her behalf." He considered it a disease in which a person is not able "to reason with oneself."[10]

[9] "Russell Brand Life without Drugs." www.theGuardian.com, March 9, 2013.
[10] Abraham J. Twerski, M.D., *Addictive Thinking: Understanding Self-Deception* (Center City MN: Hazelden, 1997), 37-38.

If indeed addictive thinking is an inability to reason with oneself, this helps to explain why successful treatment frequently follows repeated failures and setbacks on the road to recovery. On *The Big Interview* with Dan Rather, musician Gregg Allman said, "I went to 14 rehabs, but I didn't go to 15."[11] Something happened between 14 and 15 and I think that's how it often is. Something happens that forces a person to learn how to make healthy decisions and to embrace what recovery has to offer. Once, when we were checking Bobby into a rehab, one of the counselors told him he knew how to stop using heroin: he just didn't know how to stay stopped. To that, I would add that he didn't know how to want to stay stopped.

The last few years of his life, he was either depressed or slowly killing himself with drugs. Slowly killing himself was where he got the most relief. The relief was both temporary and deadly.

⬤━◆━⬤

Thought about truth
The truth may set one free from his own
outwardly, self-constructed shackles,
but not until he frees himself first from the internal mental imagery projecting
these very shackles about his ankles.
—Journal entry

---

[11] November 3, 2015.

CHAPTER THREE

The Oppressive Present

It is very hard to explain to people who have never known serious depression or anxiety the sheer continuous intensity of it. There is no off switch.
—Matt Haig, writer[12]

⎯⎯◈⎯⎯

XX

Do you believe me

When I say I'm not high

Are you preoccupied by my lies

Do I cover it

Smother it

Bury it

This love is a fire and the coals barely burn

This addiction boisterously blazes

Consuming

Controlling

No running

Or hiding

From one's own head

—Plain Songs

---

[12] Matt Haig, "Inspirational Quotes at Brainyquote," BrainyQuote (Xplore), https://www.brainyquote.com/.

I wrote the following letter as Bobby was getting ready to go to Colorado to stay with friends who understood he needed to be rescued from the temptations and connections in and around Philadelphia. To those of you who haven't read the books or seen the movies, I apologize in advance for references to *The Lord of the Rings* throughout my letters. It's similar to *Seinfeld* in that there is a scene or character that we can relate to for nearly every circumstance.

> *Dear Bobby,*
>
> *Here's your phone to confirm your appointment and call your friends. We hesitate to give it to you because it so easily connects you with the bad and the ugly, not just the good. You did not delete numbers as promised. You have long been trying to live life in two totally incompatible arenas. On one side you have family, friends, school, work and your accomplishments: the good. On the other is drugs: the bad and the ugly.*
>
> *When writer Jon Kabat-Zinn said, "Wherever you go, there you are," he was pithy and profound. Absolutely everything you found here you can find in Colorado. Some people might advise you to stay and face your demons here because the strength you need can only come from God and from within you. All Colorado really provides is distance. However, if you truly approach this as a life changing, lifesaving, fresh start that will propel you into the life you long to lead, then distance will be a blessing indeed. If you are not committed to an absolute and totally clean break from drugs and all they have come to represent in your life, then there is absolutely nowhere you can go and nowhere you can hide. Your decisions will eventually lead you down the same sorry road.*

The fact that you were, and maybe still are, willing to risk your life for drugs is alarming and evidence of their power. Many of life's dreadful decisions look attractive going in. They are reckless decisions, usually made because they address a need quickly and seemingly easily. That's why so many lives are train wrecks. People are drawn in for what looks like a fairly easy fix to their problems and life becomes Shelob's[13] web. They are alive, but completely trapped and unable to control anything that happens to them. You are standing just outside Shelob's lair. We understand that. We have been praying that God would rescue you and provide a way out and are willing to accept that Colorado may be the answer. We can let you go anywhere on this earth if it saves your life and keeps you out of the web. You need treatment and counseling, no question, no matter where you are. And it's possible that meetings and therapy may be more helpful in the calm of the Shire without the clear and present dangers associated with being on the road to Mordor. We can accept this, and God willing, healing and wholeness and a life that thrives will come to pass. This kind of life does not just happen; it takes hard work, courage, determination, resilience and faith, but the dividends are immeasurable. There are times you will need to stare down the enemy. You need to make the decisions beforehand that will give you the strength not to blink when those times come.

So, you can take Shelob with you or you can take your blessings with you. I know you don't doubt our love and support. You clearly have friends who love you immensely. The fact that Rossi and Rob are willing to take you in with your baggage speaks volumes, that's love. Erin sticking with you through all the dark times and reaching out to us when she thought you

---

[13] Shelob is a very large spider-like creature in *The Lord of the Rings* who completely incapacitates her prey by wrapping them up tightly in her web.

were in danger, that's love. Ben coming to us when he knew you were in danger, that's love. Tim offering you his couch, that's love. Ferry reaching out to you when his day-to-day life is miles away, that's love.

You can take Shelob or you can take your accomplishments with you. Your GPA and academic achievements are just waiting to be built upon. Dean's List is no small feat. And maybe your massage training will come in handy again. You leave with not just our love and support, but the love and support of your entire family. You leave with true friendships intact. These few sentences reveal a blessed life. Or you can keep Shelob with you and allow her to lurk right outside your door. To leave Shelob behind, you need to sever destructive ties now. Don't expect Colorado to do it for you.

Don't underestimate God's hand in this. Trust His promises and carry them in your heart so you are never without the Truth, never without His power. We commit to continued prayer that you will indeed find the shelter of His presence (Psalm 31:20). "For I know the plans I have for you," declares the LORD, "plans to prosper you and not to harm you, plans to give you hope and a future" (Jeremiah 29:11 NIV). Really, what more could anyone want or need? We love you more than we can say.

Mom and Dad

City of Oceans
He looks at himself in the mirror,
who is this foreigner?
Just who the hell does he think he is...?
He can never pinpoint.

So, "what's the point?" he poses to his reflection;
"All you need is a point to begin a line, project this line,
inscribe that line, be a line.
He ponders, yet is still not satisfied with the response his glass reflection poses.
—Siren Songs

I've never thought of my characters as being sad. On the contrary, they are full of life. They didn't choose tragedy. Tragedy chose them.
—Juliette Binoche, French Actress[14]

In many ways, and at many times, Bobby was full of life. He loved learning, music, art, poetry, traveling, food, football, his family, his friends, his cat. Despite this, two brutal friends, depression and anxiety, fueled his addiction. In *Seeing in the Dark*, Gary Kinnaman and Richard Jacobs write:

> ...although loss or tragedy can trigger depression, depression is much more than sadness. Like all medical conditions, depression has physical, mental, emotional and spiritual effects. When an individual becomes ill the *whole person* suffers. Depression, like asthma and diabetes, doesn't need any "reason" to occur – it just does.[15]

[14] Juliette Binoche, Inspirational Stories, Quotes & Poems, January 30, 2022, https://www.inspirationalstories.com/.
[15] Gary Kinnaman and Richard Jacobs, *Seeing in the Dark: Getting the Facts on Depression & Finding Hope Again* (Minneapolis, MN: Bethany House, 2006), 19.

They go on to say that, "... depression is not grief. It is not sadness. It is not a person feeling sorry for themselves...Major clinical depression is a disease of the "oppressive present" – we feel like we have no future. The present misery is so dominating that tomorrow moves beyond hope."[16]

The "oppressive present" and "tomorrow moves beyond hope." I believe these two quotes sum up serious depression in a way that helps those of us who have never experienced it begin to understand the sheer weight of it. I would say things to Bobby to try to give him hope for his future, things to look forward to, not realizing that his present could be so oppressive that the very future I thought would give him hope was, in his mind, actually beyond hope. There was so much I didn't know or understand. As my mom has said many times, "If love could have kept him here, he'd still be here," which, I believe, is a paraphrase of a quote by David Ellsworth in *The Serenity of Selfism* "If love could have saved you, you would have lived forever."[17] We believed our hope and love for him could penetrate an oppressiveness and a darkness that we didn't realize the depth of. I knew the seriousness of what he was dealing with because I knew all too well the manner in which he was trying to cope with it. What I didn't grasp was the depth.

Several months after Bobby died, I stumbled across a book that was useful in helping me come to terms with some of the things I had been struggling with. I was wrestling with Bobby's complicity in his death. He saw it coming and, in the end, didn't do anything to stop it. I kept wondering how this differed from suicide.

> "Suicide illness is what happens when depression grows up
> and decides to bulk up on anabolic steroids. ...Without expert
> intervention and care, the body hangs around even after the
> soul has taken flight."[18]

---

[16] Kinnaman and Jacobs, *Seeing in the Dark*, 53, 107.

[17] David Ellsworth, *The Serenity of Selfism* (Scotts Valley, CA: CreateSpace Independent Pub, 2014).

[18] Denise Norwood. Suicide Illness.pdf (stephysplace.org)/sp/Resources/Suicide/Suicide%20Illness.

Had his depression "bulked up on anabolic steroids"? Had his addiction gone from being a way to cope to being a means to an end? In some cases, are the lines between an accidental overdose and suicide so blurred they overlap? I realized the answer didn't change the outcome, or anything really, but I still wanted some clarity for my own peace of mind.

The book I found was *Making Peace with Suicide: A Book of Hope, Understanding, and Comfort*, by Adele Ryan McDowell. Specifically, it was one section of one chapter that I was interested in. The chapter was "Special Circumstances and Considerations" and the section, "Is addiction a form of slow suicide?" McDowell says that addiction "crosses a broad spectrum" and that it's not reasonable to think that all substance abuse is a form of suicide.[19]

She notes the distinctions between suicide and addiction. "Suicide is the equivalent of a shrieking alarm bell. Addiction, on the other hand, is a chronic beeping that gets louder over time."[20] For Bobby, addiction did indeed appear to have been a chronic beeping that eventually drowned out everything else. McDowell also points out areas of similarity between suicide and addiction, such as depression, anxiety and self-sabotaging behaviors. All three were long term problems for Bobby.

In another chapter, McDowell addresses the issue of connectedness as it relates to suicide. I believe this plays a large role in addiction as well. "When we find ourselves feeling like a person left without an anchor, tether, or a home base, we trudge off – be it physically, mentally, or emotionally – into a form of personal exile."[21]

One of Bobby's tattoos, across the top of his chest, was "Eloi Eloi lama sabachthani?" which is Aramaic for "My God, my God, why have you forsaken me?" These are the words spoken by Jesus on the cross, and represent, in that moment, total separation from God the Father. These words were also spoken by King David in Psalm 22:1-2 NIV "My God, my God, why

---

[19] Adele Ryan McDowell, *Making Peace with Suicide: A Book of Hope, Understanding, and Comfort* (Riverside CT: White Flowers Press, 2015), 66.
[20] McDowell, *Making Peace with Suicide*, 68.
[21] McDowell, *Making Peace with Suicide*, 75.

have you forsaken me? ...My God, I cry out by day, but you do not answer, by night, but I find no rest."

From one of Bobby's poems:

> Icy desolated deserted
> MacDade Boulevards, across lands of death
> Induce a sigh of your own breath
> Whispering
> Eli Eli lama Sabachthani

It breaks my heart that Bobby often felt so adrift and alone, so disconnected. I remember once suggesting that he pray about something and he told me that he did but his prayers weren't answered. I knew that feeling all too well, yet I don't remember what I said to him at the time. Does God heal? Yes. Do we always get what we pray for? No. Do we always get what we want when we want it? No. But God does hear and He does answer. Life and death prayers take on a depth and an urgency that prayers for everyday concerns don't have. These are the prayers that have no words, when "the Spirit Himself intercedes for us" (Rom. 8:26 NIV).

If I could have written the script, Bobby would be here, healthy, happy and thriving. This is the person whose loss is incalculable. This is the person I was praying I would see come through his addiction. This is the person I wish Bobby had fought harder to save. I still try to rewrite the script in my mind, inserting what I think I could or should have done differently to get to the ending I want. I have to admit there are times I would go back to having him here in any condition. But then, other times, I'll come across a picture or a memory in which he was going about his life obviously high. Do I wish that on him? No, but do I wish I could have him back, even in that condition, so that I could continue to try to fix things? Yes, paradoxically I do, even though all the experts tell me I can't and I know in my head they're right. But in my heart, I want him here so I can continue to try. Then I remember how much I hate heroin.

I hate what heroin did to Bobby. I hate what it did to our family and I hate that I told his sister, Hannah, that I hope she marries someone who has siblings since she's now the only surviving child. One day her future kids had an uncle, and maybe cousins, and the next day they didn't. Bobby will always be her brother. She'll always be his little sister. But there's a void that I hope others can step into. We're grateful that Bobby's friends let her know that they are there for her, not to replace him, but to simply be there if she needs them. I'm pretty sure Bobby would be the first one to say that he's irreplaceable and he would be right. And even though heroin had taken my son with it, after Bobby died there was a gradual sense of relief to be free of its influence and insidious power in our lives. It was a relief to no longer be living on high alert where even minor problems often felt like major issues. Bobby was the one who would have had to rewrite the script. No one else was in control. We did our best to help, but his days here were short, and based on the things he said and wrote, he was okay with that. God understood. When Bobby was at his weakest, in his personal exile, the following prayer was answered for him:

"O Lord, don't stay away from me! Come quickly to my rescue!"
(Psalm 22:19 GNT)

After all the darkness I have traversed
Out of all my regrets,
Regrets, regrets, regrets
That could fill a lake
I drag the lake and pick them out, one by one,
Hold them tightly but don't let them bind me.
I let them float away to the ceiling
Where they are trapped

Hovering above me

I hold my darkness close so I know its name.

I smile up to the smog above me, my regrets,

regrets, regrets

And know they cannot harm me,

For I know their names.

I count the hairs on their heads.

They are my children,

They are my teachers.

People outside of my room

Say "Let it go," but they can't truly know.

I hold on tight.

You can't know me,

But I can know myself.

—Journal entry

Bobby and Hannah, Cinque Terra, Italy

Chapter Four

The Elephant in the Room

Some never have hope-
Others keep on losing it—
Stanislaw Lec, Polish poet and aphorist[22]

⟞◆⟝

Bob wrote letters whenever Bobby was away for an extended period. Bob's letters tended to be light and encouraging, which was a nice complement to mine, which were usually more serious. Bob has been a letter writer for as long as I've known him. He's very good at keeping in touch, which I've always admired because I'm just the opposite. I'll compose letters in my head but never actually get around to writing them, which is a regret.

The following excerpts were written by Bob when Bobby was in Colorado in 2014:

> *2/18/14*
> *Hi Bobby,*
> *We truly miss you, yet are thankful that you have decided to get away and start a new chapter of your life. We are very proud of you, getting yourself to CO, and now this side trip to CA. It will be interesting to see where you lay down some roots—hope-fully East of the Mississippi and North of the Equator. So many*

---

[22] Stanislaw J. Lec, *Unkempt Thoughts* (New York: St. Martin's Press, 1965).

options. *Work hard on your studies, but not at the expense of your Recovery, which is even harder I imagine.*

Remember to reach out for support as you have a lot on your schedule. As you move ahead, keep in mind that support is only a phone call away. It's only a prayer away as well. Don't be shy or too proud to ask for help.

We will continue to pray for you each morning and each evening. Always keep in mind, "Just for today." We love you, miss you, and are looking forward to hearing about your travels.

You are loved!

Mom & Dad xoxo

3/3/14

Hi Bobby,

I still don't text (my new phone is still in its box) so I'll be old fashioned and use ink and a note card.

Hope you are well, enjoying your studies and managing the new job. Hannah and mom spent the afternoon looking up places to stay and visit this summer. Both were off today as Widener was closed due to snow. Mom just mentioned to me she was quite impressed with a poem you just posted. Me too. "So far, far away, yet forever inside." Great line. Keep writing and poeting! Be smart, be safe, be strong!

Just for today,

Love, Dad xo

3/25/14 email from Bob to Bobby:

Hi Bob, I've been thinking about you and praying you are well. You sound good on the phone. Mom and I are getting that travel bug as summer draws near. We have some hurdles, but they are not insurmountable. Be good to yourself. Stay clean and sober and all will be well with you. Not "pie in the sky" well, rather "ham where you am." My own creative writing. I bet you never heard such. It goes back to my own college days. Be good. All my love, Dad xxoo

Email from Bobby back to Bob:

Don't focus on the pie in the sky
For it will only bleed you dry
Simply trust God to unveil the blind
Removing the worldly disguise
Delivering you the prize
Ham where you am.
Ha! just what I thought of spur of the moment. Love your play on words, and love you!
I know money is tough but I know we can do it, we all only live once and I will die before I let this opportunity pass us by. I will see you in Europe if it is the last thing I do. I want nothing more than to see Geneva where you married mommy and began this amazing life that is mine. I love you so much and miss you so much. Keep writing 😊

Hi Bobby,

Miss you and love you! Going on 4 months. I'm proud of your ability to make a go of it in Colorado. Keep moving ahead while putting time and distance between you and the lure of drugs. Continue to heal and grow healthier.

You mean so much to me and mom. We are still working on the details of this summer's trip to Europe and visit to Geneva with you and Hannah.

Bob, I am so very proud of you. We feel so blessed to have a son and daughter like you and Hannah. Be hopeful, be positive, be good.

We had lunch with grandmom today after church. She sends her love.

Love, Dad xoxo

Trying marijuana maintenance
Trying therapeutic intervention
Trying geographical relocation
Trying to be happy
A pale king in the end, a peasant feeling sappy
He writes
He fights
To the bitter end I see too many loved ones send
letters from the grave they dug for themselves
An addiction which cannot bend and always leaves them broken.
These letters represent a token of hope to overcome dope, from beyond this temporal transient world
He receives these letters.
Don't give up! Don't give in!
Written in beautiful otherworldly cursive.
—Journal entry

I wrote the following letter in May of 2014 as Bobby was making plans to drive home from Colorado with a friend before leaving for London to study abroad about a week later.

> *Dear Bobby,*
> *It's hard to believe you'll be on your way home soon. I can't wait to see you. When you left, I was so happy for the rescue and relief. I was just glad you were in a safe place. Then I was terrified at the thought of you coming back. Now I'm good, but want you to think back to the day you left for Colorado before you leave*

there to come back home. When you're driving across Kansas, you'll thank me that I'm giving you something to think about. Trust me on that.

There is an elephant in the room. And since we haven't seen you in four months, we have no idea how big the elephant is. Of course, the elephant is drug use. In retrospect, it seems that you began to spiral downward pretty quickly after returning from Germany last summer. I have no way of knowing whether you went looking for it, or were overcome by triggers, but what I do know is that over the course of the fall semester, you went from a downward spiral to a death spiral. This is not meant to be melodramatic. The acceleration was dramatic. We realize now that the only thing holding you up was our foundation. Those days are over.

We feel it's imperative that you move forward and have something to build on, but you can't do that in any meaningful way while continuing to use. One of the really sad outcomes of addiction is that when people get clean, they realize that they have been suspended in time. They return to sobriety trying to make up for that lost time and realize that their friends and the world have moved on. This can be overwhelming and may contribute to the number of people who overcome addiction but can't sustain it. We didn't want this to happen to you.

Another reason to continue to support you was to give you time to work through the reasons you use. They are compelling reasons or you wouldn't have been willing to sacrifice so much in order to continue. Drugs are your enemy, as sure as someone holding a gun to your head is your enemy. Unless you know why that person wants to kill you, you'll never be able to talk him out of pulling the trigger. Whatever the reasons are that you use, there are remedies, but they don't come looking for you. You have to be proactive or you will again be overwhelmed at some point, probably at several points. Again, drugs are your enemy. You have to arm yourself against them or they will sneak up on you and destroy you. It's not easy, nor is it rocket science. A lot is common sense but many people never figure it out. We didn't want this to happen to you.

You need to think about how you're going to handle the week at home before you get here. Don't let other people make your decisions for you. If you keep company with friends with whom you have drugs in common, then you are setting yourself up for a massive derailment. That plane to London is leaving on June 2nd, whether you're on it or not. Now is not the time to try to help anyone but yourself.

This world has both good and evil. There is no escape from temptation. However, God always provides a way out. You've been given a huge safety net that has only grown larger over the past several months. The only way for it to fail you is if you yourself cut a hole in the bottom and fall out.

Jeremiah 15:20 NIV "I am with you to rescue and save you." God has proven this to be true in a very real way in your life over the past four months. We love you immeasurably and can't wait to see you. XOXOXOXOX to infinity and back, Mom and Dad

Bobby did make it to London in the summer of 2014.

June 15, 2014
Hi Bob,
Thanks for the Father's Day greeting by e-mail. It's an honor to be a father, and a blessing. I'm not sure I deserve such a wonderful marriage and beautiful children. Amazing Grace!

I am happy to hear London is suiting you as well as the internship. I wonder if we'll be able to visit the site of your internship? Our plans for Geneva and Venice have come together the past few days as we've booked places to stay.

There's a song I hear regularly and want to encourage you to check out. It's called "Untitled Hymn" by Chris Rice. It's become one of my favorites and leads me to tears almost. You must miss the fresh air of Colorado. Keep us posted. Write, text, e-mail. Looking forward to hearing from you. Take good care of yourself.

With Love,

Dad xo

Bobby and me in London

Following London, he went back to Colorado, enrolled in school for the fall semester and Bob continued to write.

10/27/14

Hi Bob,

Miss you. Love you! I know it must be hard to be so far away from home, especially when you need a hug or some encouraging words. It's always good to hear your voice when we call. I still haven't succeeded in getting or sending text messages. I'll aim to accomplish this feat by Thanksgiving. I wish you could make it here for some turkey, but this will make Christmas that much more special.

Bob, I am proud of you and want to commend you in doing what needs to be done to stay focused and on track in pursuing an education, staying clean and sober, and making the most of the opportunities that have come and will continue to come your way. Again, understand what it means to "seek first His kingdom and His righteousness." First things first, take care of today, build your future one day at a time. Make the most of each and every class, each and every relationship. I'd enjoy hearing about your roommates. Where are they from? What are they studying? Kinds of personalities, etc.?

Love you an ocean full!

Dad xoxo

P.S. Remember Hannah's b'day this Sat. Her 20th!

Bob and Bobby in Colorado

———✦———

Nov 1st, 2015 (My little sister's birthday, this is for you Hannah)
Millennials
All us children of the millennium
awaiting an omen,
seeking out the last augury,
weaving among the boomers
who present us with a forgery.

Stay strong, my children!
We are the last missionaries,
the last lost lovers,
the rarest breed indeed,
above us a genuine gospel hovers.

Stay authentic, my friends!
Set out with unmatched veracity,
imperfection glistens these days
but we see through the deceiving fog with rectitude,
we refuse to be misled.

Steer the course, my children!
The maps made for us yield no
sensible shape or design when traced,
we create our own compass.
Forgetting north south east west,
undulating inwards with a steady pace.

We desire no recompense, only truth.
With roots above and branches below,
we capture our affections in nature's photo booth
and furrow our brows in a sordid mirror reflection.

Stay clean, my sweet princes!
Hold steadfast to the healing hope hovering above our masts,
steer this ship with steady hands,
fear not the undertow.
This voyage is long and treacherous,
but this is no ship of floating fools.

Be proud, my children!
We have sailed successfully into the millennium,
leaving in our wake the outdated systems of the past.

We are the strong
We are the brave
We are the lovers
The last of our kind.
-Siren Songs

Bobby Young is with **Hannah Young**.
Aug 6, 2014 · 👥

We out here in the Alps simply stuntin with the moo moos.

Bobby and Hannah in Switzerland in 2014

Hannah and Bobby, Munich

This letter was written following the fall semester as Bobby was making plans to come home for Christmas.

> *Dear Bobby,*
> *I'm writing before you come home because your 10 days here*
> *in May did not go well. I'm not sure if we're expecting this guy –*

> *who makes the best of things. He's his own friend.*
> *Or this guy –*

who says that all that matters to him is getting to London, but lives his life in such a way that by the time that day comes, he doesn't care. He is his own saboteur. Many people who had just helped with your flight and visa would have put you out on the side of the road. But we committed to you that we will help you move forward however we can and have not wavered in that commitment. So, we put you on the plane and hoped for the best. This picture may not fully depict how miserable you were when it was taken, but we all know you were in bad shape when you left.

Life is all about the choices we make. When we make those choices, we also choose the consequences, good or bad. The consequences of bad choices are not always immediate, but when we risk them, we are accepting them. When an addict risks an overdose, which they do every time they use an uncontrolled substance, they also choose the consequences of their behavior for those who love them. Death from an accidental overdose diminishes and saddens every future birthday, every holiday, and every happy event. Forever. The loss doesn't go away. It leaves parents, grandparents, siblings and friends struggling to find meaning in the death of someone they loved.

This time last year, you were hanging on to go into rehab. You left rehab with a poor prognosis and were offered a way out. You were blessed with Durango, Fort Lewis College, your internship in London, Leeds, Riomaggiore, Venice, and you know I could go on. All of these provide the type of joy that fulfills, enriches, and endures.

You have experienced both types of high, the real and the counterfeit. The high from drugs is quick, overwhelming, and deadly, whether incrementally or all at once. It makes you want more of what will destroy you. It's dark, ugly and can make you regret it for the rest of your life.

The high from a life well lived, music, art, travel, museums, nature, the love of family and friends, the love and mercy of God, is a celebration of all that is good. It leads to a life of fulfillment. It may not always be easy, but there is no other way to happiness. Trying to avoid the pain of life does not lead to happiness. Pursuing happiness leads to happiness.

There was a recent Hillsdale College "Imprimis" article by a British guy writing about the underclass and how government worldview contributes to it. He spent a bit of time on heroin addiction for which he has no sympathy. But I actually find his honesty and lack of political correctness refreshing and hopeful. I'm not convinced he's entirely correct, but new viewpoints are always welcome. He doesn't believe that addicts are "the helpless victims of something beyond their own control. It is something they do, rather than something that happens to them."[23] I think it's possible that heroin can begin as "something they do" and then turn into "something that happens to them." He believes current treatment models lead to "a pattern of life."[24] I believe your fight to go to Colorado was a fight to gain back control of your life and to try to move beyond the addiction, not with the addiction. You knew you desperately needed to change the pattern of your life, which was a sign of wisdom and maturity in the midst of a crisis and we admire you for that.

We agree with both the Hillsdale guy and the disease model that your life and future are at the mercy of the choices you make. Taking responsibility is empowering. Making the right choices puts us in places that we wouldn't trade for the world. Drugs put people in a place where they sell their souls for the opportunity to self-destruct.

You've chosen both types of high. And you've lived the consequences of both. The consequences of good choices get better with

---

[23] Anthony Daniels, "The Worldview that Makes the Underclass," *Imprimus*, June 2014, 43.
[24] Daniels, "Worldview."

time. The consequences of bad choices get worse over time. No one can choose for you. So please choose wisely. I'll leave you with this. You came very close to seeing that neither of the following pictures was ever taken. Do you want a life with more of these or a life where the canvas is blank? Again, up to you.

We love you immeasurably. See you soon!

Love, Mom and Dad XXXOOO

CHAPTER FIVE

I Hate That It Ended

Keep me in your heart for a while
Hold me in your thoughts,
take me to your dreams
Touch me as I fall into view
When the winter comes,
keep the fires lit
And I will be right next to you
—Warren Zevon

Throughout his life, Bobby always had friends. By the time he was an adult, he had some very good ones. Some were long-standing and some were new, many of whom we know helped him carry on as long as he did. One of the things that worked against him was that he didn't always treat himself as he would treat a friend. Bob, Hannah and I have been impressed, comforted and heartened by how meaningful his relationships could be, even if he only knew someone for a short amount of time.

Nearly a year after he died, Hannah received the following message from a friend Bobby made during a short-term study abroad in Germany. The friend had just heard about Bobby's death and tracked Hannah down to let her know how much he had enjoyed knowing him.

Hello Hannah, Me and Bobby met in Greifswald and became good friends there. He revisited Greifswald later and stayed for a night at my place, it was great to catch up with him. Maybe he told you about his half German, half Syrian friend. He would write me later from time to time on facebook, but as time went by, our contact thinned down a bit. We planned that I would come over for a visit to the states once I finish my degree; he was excited to introduce me to the alternative music scene of his place. We also joked on opening a kebab doner place in the states. I just discovered that he passed away since last October. I am so sorry for your loss. I just want to tell you that your brother had such a charisma, whenever he would set foot in a room in Greifswald, he would immediately become the centre of it, everybody liked him! You surely know that better than me, you could talk with bobby on all kinds of stuff, music, literature, art, games, life, you name it. He was a very cool guy and easy going to hang out with and I would have loved to hang out with him again someday...The time I spent with him was relatively short, but I remember him much better than most of the other persons I used to hang out with, and that tells a lot about bobby! Your brother was not only loved in the States, but also in Germany. I hope you are doing well. Kind regards.

Germany 2013

Following is the Eulogy for Bobby's Memorial Service written by a longtime best friend, Michael Ferry. Michael and Bobby met during their sophomore year of high school. Mike was in Europe when Bobby died and I asked if he would write a few words for the Memorial Service Program. What he wrote is below. Hannah read it at the service.

I've known Bob since his first day at Cardinal O'Hara High School in 2004 when I invited him to sit with me at my lunch table, needless to say we've been best friends ever since. I've never known a more interesting person in my entire life and that could never change. The life that he was able to live was so much more than a movie, so much deeper than a novel, and much more profound than the longest string of stories we could all collectively tell. The amount of brilliance that he fit into his time with us (especially with his long internal struggle), the places he was able to go, the activities he was able to be part of, the amount of people he touched, is all simply amazing, especially for a Delco kid from Cheddar (Chester) as he used to call it when we first met and we rocked the shape up.

I've never known more about someone, and had someone know more about me, than him. The times we had together and how much we made each other laugh will never be matched. We went through the great times, the tough times, and loved and fought like a traditional old school married couple, always together. He was truly an amazing friend and more than I could've ever asked for when it all comes down to it. He was such an infectious soul. The way that I saw people gravitate towards him, and the way he was able to galvanize groups of people, and will continue to do so even now, is such a gift that I don't know that he ever truly or fully realized that he had, how deep it went, and just how amazing he was, no matter how much I tried to beat it into him. He inspired so many people and made us all feel important and special. He has made the world a better place and blessed us all with everything he was.

So, to my dearest best friend, although you have truly broken my heart, I am so fortunate and forever grateful to have had you for as long as I can say that I have. Thank you so much for everything that you have given me and have done for me. Our friendship has always meant, and will always mean, the world to me. I love you so very much and I will never stop missing you and the laughter we've shared over the dumbest random things. I've never laughed more than when we got going on our rants, run-ons, and inside jokes. You always knew how to make me feel special and confident. No other man could ever make another man feel better about themselves than Bob Young. We know and understand each other so well that I will forever have a void in my life and in my heart that will never be filled now that you can no longer be with me in the physical form. I've never loved another guy the way that I unconditionally love you. I truly don't know what I'm going to do without you, but I will continue to push forward like you would want me to, and look forward to the day we can speak again, play basketball again, play beer pong again, get on the sticks again, and when I can show you what-ever the latest music is that I'm on. My love is forever, Hossman Bossman, and we'll catch up soon enough, but until then I hope you can now see the shirt that I bought for us in Amsterdam last Thursday since you said you wanted it to be a surprise. We won't be able to twin it like the massive idiots that we've always been together, but we will certainly be together when I wear it in our name. You will always be here with me through the way that we have shaped each other since kids, and I will forever carry us together as one.

Finally, the flowers are thrown at your feet, but they've always been there for the things you've done. Rest easy my second brother, my best friend, and so much more. You've been tired for so long and I appreciate you staying up for as long as you have. You're in a better place now Brody, and you are finally free, but don't be a stranger. Turn loose and enjoy the new pond, Duck Sauce.

Bobby Young

Bringing in #2017 having a nice quiet dinner with the one man who's been there for me through thick and thin and always had my back since #2004 ferry you don't even have a Facebook so you wont see this but I love you #brothers

DECEMBER 31, 2016

Michael Ferry and Bobby

Jean Baptiste Prayer
Things you need that are hard
to find.
There, over there, is a disease, it waits outside,
Inside, groaning, please, please come and play, come and play.
Forget about anyone and everyone you love.

Lubricious, concupiscent
There are things that are not that easy
to find.
Say love, friendship, an absence of pain,
a feeling of hope, unfueled by any dope,
A monster which waits outside
while you groan and moan for these things

not that easy to find.

There are things that are easy
to find.
A blade of grass, a crumbling building, war, hate and malice.
Yet look harder, and you may also easily find beauty.
—Journal entry

———⊰●⊱———

We are so thankful to Bobby's friends who sent us kind sentiments after he died and will always treasure them:

> "He was one of the most outgoing and charismatic people I have ever met. He was the most incredible person many people will ever meet. He was eager to include everyone and always ensured even the strangest of people felt comfortable and at home around him."

> "You raised one of the most amazing men I have ever known in my entire life. He's a light in everyone's life who knew him."

> "I'm so proud of the loyal, compassionate, beautiful human being Bobby was."

We've often heard the word "charisma" used in connection to Bobby. One of the most unexpected times was when Bob and I went for a family counseling session when Bobby was in rehab. Before he came into the room, we asked his counselor how Bobby was doing and the counselor said he was charismatic. I still remember it because it wasn't at all the answer I was anticipating.

Bobby was pretty adept at forming friendships and making connections. When he went to hear a speaker who was involved in the arts in a meaningful and dynamic way in the local community, he wanted to be a part of that. His idea was to bring music, namely rock, to Chester, a small under-resourced city near Philadelphia. The speaker was Devon Walls, of The Artist Warehouse and Chester Made[25], who owns the MJ Freed Theater in Chester. Devon originally had his doubts about whether or not his space was the right venue, but because Devon is who Devon is and Bobby was who he was, they connected and made it happen. It was sometimes a challenge to get people from outside of the city to come to listen to music on a Saturday night, but Bobby pressed on and wouldn't take no for an answer. To his credit, he knew when something transformational was happening. He knew when he'd found the cool people and he knew zip codes are irrelevant when it comes to art and music. He didn't seem to have a problem getting people to come play. In fact, he found some incredible musicians and artists to perform in an inviting and creative space made possible by artistic, visionary people. I continue to be amazed by how thankful they were to be there despite the fact that they came for gas money at best and played for a small audience.

Chester, PA

---

[25] https://chestermade.org.

We always knew Bobby tended to get around. So, several months after he died, we weren't too surprised when Bob's sister, Dottie, called to let us know that Bobby's picture had been used on a blog post and she wanted to make sure we didn't mind. We found the blog, and at the end, the writer noted:

> That cool Widener guy does not represent the essence of this article (white privilege). He was one of the only young white man photos I had on my computer. For the purposes of this post, let's just call him a faceless nameless model. I hope he doesn't mind.[26]

Bobby was able to make connections everywhere so no one who knew him would be surprised that he would be the random "young white man" in somebody's photos. No, he wouldn't have minded. In fact, I'm sure he'd have been happy to help and would have been flattered to be the model.

---

[26] "Chester Matters Blog" (Wordpress.com, February 17, 2019), https://chesterpablog.wordpress.com/2019/02/17/young-white-men-have-it-bad.

Of course, all of the positive comments don't give a complete picture of dealing with Bobby, as anyone who has dealt with addiction knows. There were also the following phone calls, Facebook posts and texts:

"I'm worried about Bobby."

"I'm sorry I wish I could have done something more to help but I don't think I can help him like he believes I can. Only he can do that...I just hope."

"I'm with him now. I just don't want him out of my site."

"He wanted to test everything, but that's not how it works. Not everything can be tested."

"Amazing people have demons too. Sobriety was exhausting for him. The struggle has been constant for years."

"This is just an outrage to me. He'll never learn."

"Bobby THREW himself constantly so deep into a flaming existence in all ways – and he has been smacking himself against the edge since I've met him. He has been chasing his dreams the best that he could with everything he had within. He had so much to share and say and feel. I hate that it ended. I have always rooted for him."

<hr />

Twang
I break more guitar strings than hearts,
I am bad at music
I am bad at love.

I hit the chords too hard

I break more drum heads than hearts,

I am bad at rhythm
I am bad at love.

I strike the snare too hard.
—Journal entry

*With friends (Andrew) Rossi and (Michael) Ferry – I
never heard Bobby refer to Rossi as Andrew or Ferry
as Michael. It was always by last name.*

Bobby and friend Tim "TK" Krawiec

At the Artist Warehouse in Chester, PA. Photo credit Greg Irvin

Chapter Six

I Was Born to Hustle Roses

Wanderer

Come with me/Into the dark woods

You can't show me/Where to find truth

They said boy better get clean/Keep on using keep on dying

stuck in the soul realm

where did you snuff the light?

I cannot find it

Gotta stop playing with fire

#Butit'shardwhenthecityisburning

—Plain Songs

Bobby loved music, literature and art. His ability to find meaning in a painting made me feel as if I'd spent my life looking at art with one eye closed. We went to museums together and occasionally to concerts. One of my favorite memories was at the TLA in Philly, where we went to see Portugal. The Man. There's a large open floor downstairs and a much smaller balcony area. Bobby was down on the floor with friends. Bob and I were up on the balcony. Toward the end of the night, a young man in his thirties approached us to say that he was happy to see people as old as we were could still make it out to shows. It gave him hope for his future, so we took it as a compliment.

A significant part of the draw to music for Bobby was the lyrics. Since he was always struggling to get his bearings and to make sense of his place in the world, when he came across lyrics that reverberated with him, they were like a lifeline tossed to a drowning man. So much so that he would sometimes honor that lifeline with tattoos depicting the band.

Bobby wasn't shy about sharing his story. After he died, his struggle with addiction was included in a production for the 2019 Philly Fringe Arts Festival. Theater Oblivion and actor/singer Amanda Shaffern produced *Siren Songs*, a play designed to address the stigma surrounding addiction. Fifty people who had struggled with addiction were interviewed and seven stories, including Bobby's, were chosen for the play. Prior to the start of the show, Amanda contacted us for our permission to include some of Bobby's poetry and to let us know that they would like to call it *Siren Songs* to honor him and others who had lost the fight to addiction. Everyone connected to *Siren Songs* was gracious, warm and kind and these qualities spilled over into the production itself.

Actor and songwriter Jeremy Adam portrayed Bobby in the show, did an amazing job and said that they were sure they could sense Bobby's presence at times. Nearly a year after the play, Jeremy wrote the following on Facebook and played a song he had written for Siren Songs. When I first heard the song during the play, I was surprised that I hadn't heard or read the words before because I thought Bobby had written them. It sounded just like him.

> I never got the chance to meet him. He passed away before I even knew about the show. He was a poet. He was an artist, and a musician. I learned most of what I knew about him from a 45-minute interview and by talking with folks that knew him in life. He was loved. He affected the people around him and he wanted to understand the world. He was a traveler. He was a philosopher. He was a believer, even if he didn't exactly know what he believed. His story could've been anyone's story, and that spoke to me...
>
> The purpose of the show was to break the stigma that surrounds addiction and to open the conversation about the

current opioid crisis in this country and around the world. As creators, it's our job to tell the stories of those who need their voices to be heard. About a month and a half into rehearsing, I swear it was like he came to me as a muse and helped me write the song...

Rest in Peace and Love [27]

Lyrics to the song Jeremy referenced:

Don't tell me I'm the problem, cause I feel like I'm the problem
But the problem is the things you say tend to hold the truth
Don't tell me I've got issues, cause I know that I've got issues,
But the issue isn't what you say, it's in the things you do.

And I don't want to spend my life wondering about all that could've been
And I don't want to waste my time crying over things I never did.

So tell me that I'm crazy, cause this fucking world's gone crazy,
And the crazy things I want to say feel a lot like truth.
I'll tell you what I'm thinking, even if nobody's listening.
Maybe if I just keep singing then you'll SHOUT IT WITH ME, TOO

And I don't want to spend my time regretting all the lines I never crossed
And I don't want to waste my life crying over loves that I have lost.

---

[27] Jeremy Adam Music | Facebook

Is it me or is this room spinning?
I can't breathe, and the devil is grinning.
Feels like we're back at the beginning.
At the end, we start. When you find my heart,

Set it free; let it keep beating.
All my wounds heal. Please stop the bleeding.
Feels like we could keep on repeating.
At the end, we start. Then, we fall apart.[28]

———◆———

Rock and Hard Place
Being inclined to be a writer and fascinated with literature is so dreadfully awful because one is ever stuck between the desire to read every word ever written and to express on paper every thought one has had. There is no end, no goal and no chance of ever being satisfied.
—Siren Songs

———◆———

Another love of Bobby's was books. We have a house full of books. I love to read and Bob loves to read and to collect books so we were both happy that Bobby and Hannah loved to read as well. Bobby fell in love with *The Lord of the Rings* in elementary school. Much later, he read and loved *Infinite Jest* by David Foster Wallace. It took him a while to get through it, but in the end, he counted Wallace as one of his favorite authors. Bobby copied the following

[28] "Jeremy Adam - Siren Song," Soundcloud, https://soundcloud.com/thejeremyadam/siren-song-live-from-the-original-play-siren-songs.

quote, from another Wallace novel, *The Broom of the System,* into a notebook and I think it sums up why he related to Wallace. "I can remember being young and feeling a thing and identifying it as homesickness, and then thinking well now that's odd, isn't it, because I was home, all the time. What on earth are we to make of that?"[29] Much of Bobby's life and thinking seemed to have been asking "What on earth are we to make of that?" There was a sense of innate alienation that was likely exacerbated by the fact that most of us don't feel that way. Most of us don't feel homesick when we are, in fact, at home.

Despite this, Bobby had a good sense of humor and we enjoyed passing David Sedaris books back and forth. He also loved to read poetry and one of his favorites was Charles Bukowski. So much so that Bukowski was the source of a tattoo across his waist, "I was born to hustle roses down the avenues of the dead," from "Consummation of Grief":

> *I even hear the mountains*
> *the way they laugh*
> *up and down their blue sides*
> *and down in the water*
> *the fish cry*
> *and the water*
> *is their tears.*
> *I listen to the water*
> *on nights I drink away*
> *and the sadness becomes so great*
> *I hear it in my clock*
> *it becomes knobs upon my dresser*
> *it becomes paper on the floor*
> *it becomes a shoehorn*
> *a laundry ticket*

[29] David Foster Wallace, *The Broom of the System,* Goodreads (Goodreads, 2AD), https://www.goodreads.com/.

it becomes
cigarette smoke
climbing a chapel of dark vines...
it matters little
very little love is not so bad
or very little life
what counts
is waiting on walls
I was born for this
I was born to hustle roses down the avenues of the dead

Poetry is a way of taking life by the throat.
—Robert Frost, American poet[30]

How does one craft a word?
Is a poem created
or
did it make itself?
If you find yourself in a life raft
Stand
The water is not that deep.
—Journal entry

[30] "A Quote by Robert Frost." Goodreads, accessed September 1, 2020. https://www.goodreads.com/quotes/179203-poetry-is-a-way-of- taking-life-by-the-throat.

Bobby enjoyed both reading and writing poetry. Some of his poetry was for his own amusement, some of it was to vent, and some I believe, was to try to take "life by the throat." I knew before he died that one of his favorite poets was T.S. Eliot. Later, I came across a school assignment and learned that his favorite T.S. Eliot poem was the "The Love Song of J. Alfred Prufrock." In the assignment, Bobby wrote that the poem deals with a man reflecting on what his life has been up to that point. He may have liked it so much because he could identify with Prufrock. The poem's narrator is a man who is searching for love and meaning. Near the end a sense of longing is tangible:

> I have heard the mermaids singing, each to each
> I do not think that they will sing to me.[31]

Some of Bobby's thoughts on writing poetry from one of his journals:

I have heard stand-up comedy referred to as the rawest of art forms, for it is only the comic and his mic, his ability to connect and make people laugh. I don't disagree, however, what then of the poet? A comic's audience is there under the supposition that they will be stirred to merriment and laughter, i.e. happiness, if brief, happiness. The poet has no pretense, operates to an audience under zero supposition and must create his own world in which operate certain rules, in which to communicate with himself foremost. To the poet an audience should be an afterthought. Sure, it's good to my spirit when others recognize my work, but my own recognition is what gives me a spirit in the first place.

---

[31] T.S. Eliot, *Selected Poems* (New York: Harcourt, Brace & Company, 1964), 16.

Someone pay me for my words.
I can't eat my words.
I can't get high with my words.
I can't buy love with words, no matter how hard I try.
When walking through a graveyard,
All you see are worn, gray, sun-cracked words.
These are the saddest words there are.

Will someone please pay me for my words.
I can't eat my words.
I can't drink them.
I can't get high with them.
I can't buy love with words, no matter how I speak.
And yet, words are the most valuable thing I can create.
When strolling through a graveyard,
Among the worn smooth, sun-cracked gray are words, only words,
And these are the truest words
there are.
—Journal entry

CHAPTER SEVEN

Crossing the Rubicon

How long, My Lord, how long to sing this song?[32]

⟫—◆—◆—⟪

The following two letters were written in quick succession during the summer of 2015. In July, Bobby went to rehab and arranged with a friend to get picked up before the standard 28 days of insurance coverage was up. We didn't think leaving early was a good idea and told them as much. I spoke with his friend and she assured me that she was up to the task of dealing with someone with an addiction because she had a family history. The reality is, no one is up to the task. When he relapsed, she had his stuff on the curb before he was out of the ER. If you aren't in it for the long haul, it's not a good idea to bail someone out for the short term. He was unintentionally set up for failure, he did fail, and it just added to his sense of inadequacy.

> *Dear Bobby,*
> *Happy birthday. Every day can be a new start, a day of new beginnings, but our birthdays are special because they are personal. They are our new start, our new beginning. Twenty-six years ago Saturday you were welcomed into our family, much loved and much wanted. That hasn't changed.*

---

[32] "mewithoutYou - silencer2," Genius, accessed September 1, 2020, https://genius.com/Mewithoutyou-silencer-lyrics.

We're proud of you that you recognized you were in trouble and sought help. I understand that rehab can just serve as a time out but there is value in that. You needed a break and you got it. However, it can also provide time for reflection, planning and soul searching. Addiction, and its causes and cures, fill books. Addiction fills rehab centers. It also fills graveyards.

We recently watched a TED talk by a British journalist, Johann Hari, who studied addiction because he wanted to help his family and friends. No agenda. No book to sell. He said everything we think we know about addiction is wrong and that the opposite of addiction is not sobriety. The opposite of addiction is connection.[33] I've had to think about that. He said the addict doesn't want to be present in his or her own life. That does make sense to me. I've often wondered how anyone could give up everything for alcohol or drugs. But maybe the reality is that the addict already feels profound loss. He or she feels disconnected from his or her life and the drug is a way to deal with the loss, not the cause of the loss. And each time the addict uses, the loss becomes greater, making it harder to find one's way back. That also somewhat explains how people can go to rehab, get clean, be positive, go home and overdose. They have lost the connection to their own lives and when faced with it in an uncontrolled environment, the loss is overwhelming. Hari's was a perspective that I hadn't heard before.

Bobby, it's not just you who struggle and try to make sense of life. Everything that can be measured or felt is on a continuum and we are all someplace on that continuum. I've had days where I just wanted the pain to stop. We all go there, but that's not where we all live. Which takes me back to connectedness. It's hard to

---

[33] "Everything You Think You Know About Addiction Is Wrong." TED Talk. Accessed September 15, 2020. https://www.ted.com/talks/johann_hari_everything_you_think_you_know_about_addiction_is_wrong.

develop the good in our lives if we don't feel connected or invested in it, if we don't trust it. I don't have all the answers. But I trust in the One who does. He knows your every thought, every action, and loves and forgives you. You should do no less. Forgive yourself. Love yourself enough to give you a chance in this world. You are gifted. Getting the proper support can help you connect with those gifts and with the people you love and care about.

Love, Mom and Dad

The second letter was written in anticipation of his discharge.

Dear Bobby,

We're writing to give you the lay of the land prior to coming home. I've written letters before and am not sure how much you take my advice to heart but this one is a bit different in that it's not so much about you. It's about us.

We'll decide day to day, week to week, whether or not to allow you to stay here. We will not offer more than that because you like heroin too much. We can't compete with it, so we aren't going to try. Use and you go elsewhere.

This fall is an ideal opportunity to get your life back on track. There have been periods of time during which you set heroin aside. To reclaim and then build a life which gives you joy, satisfaction, purpose, and a sense of pride means you'll have to leave it behind. You need to meet its intensity with a sense of your own intensity. If you don't double down, if you keep the door open even a crack, based on the past, you will go through it. The older you get, the higher the stakes. We are not a revolving door. You will continue to ruin relationships. You will continue to ruin your health. You will continue to limit your future.

This is not business as usual. Thinking you can pick up where you left off with trying to give the appearance of taking recovery seriously is not an option. If places are triggers, don't go there. If people are triggers, don't contact them. If you want to go back into the drug world thinking you have it under control, go elsewhere. We're glad you see home as a stable, helpful place to be. But it's only as stable and therapeutic as you allow it to be. We're here to help, not enable. We don't regret things we've done, however, it's always hard to decide what's best. For everybody. The TED talk I spoke about in my last letter was encouraging in that he said it's important that you know you're not alone and that you know you're loved.[34] Those are two things we've always communicated to you, so our instincts aren't entirely wrong. But this is such a difficult road to navigate that I don't pretend that they've always been right either.

When you do come home, you are not an equal player. It's our house and our lifestyle, our rules. Disrupt us and you'll have to go elsewhere. I'm sure at this point you're thinking "but I have no place else to go." Honestly that's not really our problem. We can only offer so much, and we do that gladly. However, we are not offering our peace of mind. You are perilously close to a precipice. It drops you in places like Kensington. It's for people who say to Satan, 'No need to wait until I'm dead. I'm willing to live in hell now.'

Some of those people are estranged from their families. You are not.

Some of those people are without health care. You are not.

Some of those people don't have an education on which to build. You do.

Some of those people have irrevocably damaged their bodies. You have not.

Some of those people have damaged their brains to the point

---

[34] Ibid.

that they will never fully function again. You have not.

How many are surprised at how quickly they ended up there after they stopped fighting their addiction. How many have families who would give anything for them to walk away from drugs but can no longer deal with a loved one who is actively using. You would be wise to walk away from the edge. If you want to live there, go elsewhere because it would break our hearts to see you go over the cliff.

We're done with drugs. We're done with you skirting the edges of recovery without ever fully embracing it. It's well past time that you enter some serious therapy and get to the root of your problems. We are not a recovery house; we are not therapists. We are offering a safe stable place to be to embrace recovery and therapy. But if you make our environment less safe by bringing drugs back in or less stable by arguing or pushing back against any of the above, then go elsewhere and save us all the drama.

I don't think you have any idea of the impact your addiction has had on us, so let me tell you. We're in a club we don't wish on anyone. Parents who are one bad decision away from picking their kid up at the morgue. Parents whose hearts are in their throats when a number comes up on caller ID that they don't recognize. Parents who want to cry when they look at little boys and girls and long for the innocence lost. That said, we feel no condemnation. Heaven has no condemnation. Only you can get us out of this club. Only redemption and the power of Heaven can keep us out. We love you, Mom and Dad

We can pinpoint, with 100% accuracy, the day of no return. I got a call from a trauma nurse telling me that Bobby had been shot. She was extremely quick to add, "But he's okay." So quick that there was no time for panic to begin to set in. Unfortunately, less true words were never spoken. He never recovered. Not so much physically, although he had residual pain until his death eighteen months later, but what it did to him psychologically was his point of no return. It was his Rubicon. He crossed the river, and there was no going back. I don't think it had to be that way, but it was. As much as Bobby's addiction negatively impacted his relationships, he was not malicious. Addicts become master liars, manipulators and victims. He could be all three, sometimes all at the same time. He could be enthusiastic about the wrong things and made destructive decisions. But in all of this, I never knew him to be malicious. So, when he put himself in the wrong place, at the wrong time, for the wrong reason and was shot in the back, he carried that trauma with him all day every day. He never understood how someone could be so cold and callous.

My initial reaction was that now Bobby would finally see the light. He would have to acknowledge just how dangerous drugs were and how worthless his life was to anyone dealing them. He would realize the pure folly of putting himself in that position and would change his ways. Instead, he was traumatized, hurt, defeated and in pain. In fact, he sometimes dated his addiction from this incident. This was when he lost control. I came across a diagram he completed designed to connect an event with subsequent behavior. It was probably done as part of a counseling session. The event he chose was "getting shot." The consequence was "I'll never be happy again." This led to feelings of "worthlessness, self-pity and pain." The resulting behavior was "use drugs." The young man who shot him was arrested. There was no trial. There's not much you can say to a judge or jury when you shoot someone in the back.

Dealing with the hospital after this was the first time we encountered the lack of understanding that sometimes exists in how best to deal with a patient with opioid addiction. We also learned some things we were just as happy not to know. For example, when a person is shot and taken to the hospital, they are in a guarded unit. Everyone is a suspect until the shooter is caught. It was impossible to get in to see him that day, but we were able to talk to the surgeon. He told us Bobby would be in for two nights. We informed him that Bobby had an opioid addiction that needed to be considered when prescribing pain meds and would they please call us when he was discharged. As it turned out, he was released the next day without our knowledge. I can understand if Bobby didn't give the hospital permission to let us know he was being discharged, then their hands were tied by HIPAA regulations. What I didn't understand was the total lack of common-sense regarding pain meds. He was sent on his way with a packet of ten Percocet. He took nine of them on the way home.

One other time that we were completely disregarded by someone in the medical community was following an overdose. Bob was with Bobby when he was taken by ambulance to the nearest hospital. At the time, we were following the advice people were giving us to try "tough love," which meant he couldn't come home. We wanted him admitted which would give us time to find a rehab bed. Then we would give him the choice of either taking the bed or finding another option. Since he couldn't come home, we felt pretty confident that he would take the bed. Bob knew the admission would need to be involuntary and felt he had enough evidence to convince a judge that Bobby was indeed a danger to himself and needed enforced inpatient care. The judge agreed. Bob came home only to find out that the psychiatrist on duty did not agree. We called the hospital social worker several times and pleaded with her to let the psychiatrist know that Bobby had nowhere to go upon discharge and that we would find a rehab bed for him when places opened in the morning. At this point it was after midnight. The psychiatrist told the social worker that he had talked to Bobby who convinced him he was fine. We then asked her to relay to him that, first of all, addicts will lie in order to avoid admission and the psychiatrist should know this, and second, Bobby could charm the birds out of the trees. It was to no avail. He was discharged, in the middle of the night, in December, with no coat, no money and no place to go. By this time, Bob and I had turned off the lights, locked the door and gone to bed. Bobby managed to talk his way onto public transit to get back to our neighborhood from the other end of the county. A bus driver had more mercy on him than a person employed by an institution founded by the

Sisters of Mercy. One never knows where one's angels will be found. The next morning, our instincts were telling us we should find him. Bob found him unconscious in a nearby park. If he had not found Bobby when he did, we very likely would have lost him then. Our experiences with tough love were like walking a tightrope with someone who didn't care whether or not he fell off. It's hard to let someone fall when that person doesn't care whether or not there's a net. In fact, there were times when he hoped there wouldn't be a net. That said, sometimes tough love is the solution. For instance, one of the people working in recovery that we met along the way said his turning point was when his mom kicked him out of the house and told him he could never live there again. It was his catalyst for change. As my friend Tom once told me, when I really needed to hear it, "This is such an impossible situation that whatever you do is right."

Since losing Bobby, we've had our hearts broken again by the death of a friend we believe was also improperly evaluated by a member of the medical community. Substance abuse is a frustrating diagnosis to work with. It's an even more frustrating diagnosis to live with, especially when you factor in mental health disorders. When our friend arrived in an ER he needed help, needed to be protected from himself and needed time in a safe environment in order to come back to his senses. Instead, he was regarded as being manipulative and was discharged onto a collision course with himself.

Not everyone who needs help willingly accepts it. Sometimes that decision needs to be made by others, even if they can only enforce it temporarily. The medical community classifies addiction as a disease, then too often treats people as if it's a moral failure or behavioral shortcoming. Trying to have it both ways costs lives.

<hr />

I live in a world, where
I have been shot, by multiple definitions
Some shots to kill
Some shots to numb
Some shots to save
A gun by a 17-year-old kid almost killed me
Stitched up and on the streets again, the next day
Only to last one week
To be saved by another kind of shot
The cure for the poison that plagues
My street and my generation
Why are the illegal drugs so easy to get
Why are guns so easy to get
Why are some evil
And why is there not an abundance of love
Not a poem, an outcry
—Journal entry

CHAPTER EIGHT

Bring the Beauty Back

I awake so desperate most mornings
It is pitiful when all that is on
my mind is death. I have an easy life.
But I broke my brain.
But I broke my brain.
I want to cover myself in dirt
and
never be seen again.
Florida is far from Philly.
Germany is even farther from Philly.
China is on the opposite side of our marble from Philly.

Nowhere is far enough.
Pick me up and keep driving.
I shaved the sides of my head
You shaved one side of yours
Trying to get closer to my mind.
I Ching
Tarot
The Bible

There are so many ways out of
a living grave.
I just need a hand to grab me.
I just need a body to hold me.

Uncover this dirt from my eyes
so I can see the beauty all
around me.
Wash my eyes
so I can see the beauty
all around me.
I am seeing the world through
dirt
dirt
crust
covered glasses.
Take them off my face,
kiss my cheek
and tell me everything will be
ok.
Bring the Beauty Back
Bring the Beauty Back
—Journal entry

I wrote the following letter in response to hearing about yet another death caused by an overdose. Two years later, we would be on the other side of this conversation.

2016

Hi Bobby, I'll see you at lunch but sometimes I have to put my thoughts down on paper because they become overwhelming. I'm sure you've seen the latest overdose death because you are connected by facebook friends. I think he was 22. His family said he didn't want help anymore. He was possessed by a drug and let a momentary high trump everything he once held dear. It's tragic, heartbreakingly sad, an enormous waste of potential, and at this point in the heroin epidemic, it's also a special kind of stupid. I know the first three points are what's usually emphasized, and don't quote me on the fourth, because I know how cold and heartless it sounds. His brother said it just takes over and I don't presume to argue that. But it can be overcome because it has been overcome. Everyone knows where continued use leads. I don't know if we're waiting for you to die or if we're waiting for you to live. What I do know is that when your emotions have been highjacked to the point that you are willing to make a life-or-death decision with all the coping and decision-making skills of the average toddler, then you need to stop making this decision based on how you feel. Look at what heroin does. You owe it to yourself to try to be objective. It entices you with a momentary sense of completely artificial bliss which leads straight to hell on earth. It convinces you that you are worthless, whoever sells it to you confirms your worthlessness, so then you want to use even more to escape yourself. You have a soul. You can never escape yourself, either in this world or the next.

More than anything, we want you here. We want you clean. We want you to reclaim your life. I know you value our love and support; however, we can't do it for you. We don't know where this is going. All the families who will forever grieve the loss of a child, sibling, etc. to drugs would go back and keep trying to save that person from themselves, from the drugs. So far, that has been our story and I thank God you are still here. Only God can truly revive.

I will say it again. You're either spiraling up or spiraling down. Home is for spiraling up, for putting your recovery first and getting on your feet. People make their choices. The young man who just died made his. You need to make yours. I love you.

And when I die, remove my heart, I want to know if any love is present.

And when I pass, remove my lungs, I want to know if any breath is left.

If, as The Bard said, "all the world's a stage" and we are "merely players" in a farce, when my heart ceases to beat, let me know if a curtain drops.

—Journal entry

Hannah, Bob and Bobby, Christmas 2016

Two years before he died, Bobby wrote a letter that reads like a suicide note. In fact, that's what I thought it was when I found it after he died, but half way through he mentioned that he was turning 27. Although his intent was clear, he lived another two years. The letter began with "Why?" As Friedrich Nietzsche said, "He who has a why to live can bear almost any how." Bobby then went on to say that there was not much left to do in this life of any real wonder, beauty or intrigue. "I want to die young." He said he was eternally bored and asks, "What is there really to latch onto, each other? Yes! Absolutely I regret leaving before you, I see the cowardice, the vanity and self-loathing. I live with these negative soul suckers daily... I feel no permanence here and feel detached from my own life...I feel like a spectator awaiting the curtain to close at a semi-exciting theatrical performance."

He went on to say he was sick of letting his parents down, that this "killed him" more than anything and was an insurmountable regret. He said he was sorry and felt that he had to apologize for the way he was his whole life. As Bobby got older and we became increasingly aware of just how negative his self-talk was, we became desperate to help him counter it. We encouraged him, bought books and got him to counseling. He said he always felt this way, but the destructive negativity didn't truly manifest until he was in his late teens.

As a child, we were aware that he was dealing with attention deficit disorder which was later confirmed by testing. When he was about 2 or 3, I remember playing a game with him we called "Straight-line Bobby" in which he would be rewarded for doing what we asked him to do without getting side-tracked. This was always a challenge. Then on a trip to New York City, when he had just turned twelve, I felt as if I'd been given a glimpse into his psyche in a whole new way. He was standing in the middle of Times Square looking as if he were home. I remember thinking that it may have been the first time in his life that there was more going on outside his head than in it. He was simply mesmerized. When, years later, I asked him what led him to drugs in the first place, he said he needed to stop all the stuff going on in his head. It was something he was never able to get a handle on.

While I do believe Bobby felt the need to "stop all the stuff going on in his head," I think there had to be more to his behavior than that. In *Night Falls Fast: Understanding Suicide* by Kay Redfield Jamison, she states that people with substance abuse disorders have the third highest risk of suicide, after previous suicide attempt and mood disorders. In the book, Jamison discusses the importance of biology in our response to the world around us. Our genes primarily determine our temperaments and our temperaments influence the decisions we make and how we react to and are affected by the world around us.[35]

She also references the "two-hit" model as it relates to illness in general and to suicide in particular. According to this model, having a predisposition for an illness doesn't mean it will definitely occur. But adding behavioral or environmental stressors, a second "hit," could make it more likely. This leads me to question whether this also holds true for addiction. Did Bobby's genes predispose him to addiction? Then did an impulsive, sometimes reckless temperament provide the second "hit"? Or was he simply self-medicating to "turn off his brain" and to alleviate anxiety and depression? He once wrote from a rehab facility, "now here I am, hopefully someone here can help me be me without drowning in substances to numb myself." In any case, once he made the decision that drugs were an option, street drugs were easy to find and difficult to stop.

In his letter, Bobby went on to say, "So, of course, I am sorry for a final time. Just know I am now free and hope the positive energy I did have can live on, that in my story people will glean hope and understanding." Bobby did have positive energy which seems like an oxymoronic

---

[35] Kay Redfield Jamison, *Night Falls Fast* (New York: Alfred A. Knopf, 1999), 196-197.

description given so much of what he wrote. At his memorial service we had several poster boards with pictures. Following the service, I overheard someone note that he was smiling in most of the pictures, which is true. A former teacher mentioned that she had recently run into him and he seemed happy and pleased to see her, which I'm sure he was. Two people came up to us at an event, after Bobby died, to tell us that they knew him and they each talked about him with a smile. I remember thinking that I hope I'm remembered that way. With a smile.

Bobby was most happy when he was around other people. He could be jammed in a gritty Philly basement listening to music with his friends one weekend and in Annapolis with his Grammy and us, reading *Lord Jim* in the park the next. His tastes, activities and interests were eclectic; he didn't have a well-defined lane. When he would occasionally consider teaching English abroad, once he finished his degree, he would talk in terms of all of us going with him. We didn't start taking Vietnamese lessons, but we were touched that it was natural for him to want to do things together.

He wasn't just remembered with a smile in the US. Bobby did a short-term study abroad at a Chinese university during his sophomore year of college. When Hannah followed three years later and met students who had known Bobby, they always remembered him with a smile and a story. But this dichotomy in his approach to life added to the confusion. We knew he was struggling, but the fact that he could readily rebound and seemingly enjoy so many different facets of life gave us hope that sobriety would win out. We hung onto that.

But sadly, by the end of his life, the soundtrack in Bobby's head had become a continual source of dread, fear and anxiety. He would tell us that the first thing in the morning, before he even had a chance to gather his thoughts, the negative judgements would begin and then continue throughout the day. In an article entitled, *Philip Seymour Hoffman is another victim of extremely stupid drug laws*, Russell Brand wrote, "There is a predominant voice in the mind of an addict that supersedes all reason and that voice wants you dead. This voice is the unrelenting echo of an unfillable void."[36] I can't imagine what it's like to live with that voice in my head, but I do know how devastating and heartless it is. We would talk to Bobby about that voice and tell him it was possible to turn it off. We would point out that people have successfully turned it off and that this was essential in order to have any chance at a sustainable recovery.

Just as I couldn't relate to the depth of his depression, I also didn't share the intensity of his anxiety. Bobby knew I couldn't relate, but to his credit, he would listen to me when I tried to encourage him and would try to help me understand anyway. In a journal he wrote, "The minute I open and am out my front door, it is a war." After he died, I read the following poem written by our friend Liz Baronofsky, who does understand anxiety and what it feels like to be "on the verge of an internal combustion." Although Liz can relate to some of what Bobby felt, real beauty and hope lie in her ending, "My world will not blow up in front of me...Because today I'm winning and tomorrow I will win again."

Thump thump thump thump.

I sit as every single fear pounds on my chest wall
The room around me spins
And everyone seems to be reaching for my attention
But I can't hear anything over this beating heart
Begging for mercy

It has a voice
But its sound waves travel like a bag of bricks
that wind up sitting on my chest
I can no longer formulate words
I'm captivated by the deafening noises inside my head

---

[36] Russell Brand: Philip Seymour Hoffman Is Another Victim of Extremely Stupid Drug Laws." The Guardian (Guardian News and Media, February 6, 2014), https://www.theguardian.com/commentisfree/2014/feb/06/russell-brand-philip-seymour-hoffman-drug-laws.

Telling me that I can no longer live like this anymore
And there's an obligatory inability to stop
connecting with the world around me
When I can barely hold the world inside me together

But maybe that's the problem
Maybe I'm disconnecting pieces that should have just been whole
How do you mend something that was never broken
But formulated within your molecular being
Because everything comes down to a science
And now we are here
And the world just is
Because of specific combustions that happened
within a perfect moment in time
Yet I can't seem to figure out why I can't breathe most of the day
When there is nothing physically wrong with my being
Just my brain

I can't explain why I can see things happen in my
mind before they happen in real time
And I can't describe what it feels like to have those ghostly hands
Wrapped tight around my throat
For part of my day daring me to speak above their squeeze
But I refuse to go down like this

Thump thump thump thump.

Sometimes my heart is pounding so hard that I
wonder if people around me can hear it
I wonder if they know my head is screaming
for mercy with my lips sealed shut
I wonder if I will ever truly make sense of this

And all of the fears that stole my innocence
Before I knew what being innocent was

Why I used to sleep on the floor of my closet
with the doors barricaded shut
Why I was too scared to ever really close my eyes
Why I never felt comfortable in my own skin

But I stopped hiding a long time ago
And I wear my skin more proudly than ever
I broke out of my shell and stepped into a new
set of shoes that I'll never take off

And even though I'm on the verge of an internal combustion
Almost every single day
My world will not blow up in front of me
And the thump thump thumping can keep knocking
And I'll keep listening
Because today I'm winning and tomorrow, I will win again[37]

---

[37] Liz Baronofsky@wage_the_war

CHAPTER NINE

Elegant Decay

Elegant Decay
OR
(pale horses with You)
where did all the dreams go?
once soaring
over river sea desert arctic ocean
roots and veins
deserted glistening ringing
over yellow, red and purple
poppy fields temptations' shimmering
now I am souring
I ate the forbidden fruit
and rather than being sweet
it was sour.

where did all the dreaming go?
I recall traversing convoluted causeways
unconscious
uncontrollably wandering then falling
toothless
standing amidst the spider king
I ask if I can bring a date to the wedding
the king replies, 'No, and I hath stolen the ring!
You must sing for me, lest be spun and forever left undone.'

and rather than being sweet,
it was sour.

where did all the dreams go?
I recall traveling charging at the one
the one was forever in my view.
I challenged the one
cross-eyed concupiscent cyclopean nightmare,
the siren song always draws me in
and rather than being sweet,
It is sour.
I wake up and think, rather than say,
are we all not just elegant decay?
—Siren Songs

The following letter was written when Bobby was in a rehab in South Carolina in January 2018. In his early and even mid-twenties, he was able to stay clean for long periods of time. But by 2016 - 2017, especially after he was shot in 2016, his drug use was accelerating. December was often a tough month for him. I would remind him that he couldn't maintain having one foot in the sober world and one in the drug world forever. He had to choose or the drugs would choose for him. But until shortly before he died, he was still somehow able to keep moving forward, adding university credits, traveling, not burning too many bridges in a way that was pretty remarkable. And I still kept warning him that it was unsustainable, thinking that when forced to choose, he would choose sobriety. Because that's what I would do. I remember once telling him that if he had just listened to me from the beginning, he could have saved himself a lot of trouble. Without even stopping to think, he said, "But then I'd be you, not me." Touché Bobby, touché. I miss exchanges like that. But he never really did choose. He let the drugs choose for him.

January, 2018
Dear Bobby,

We're sorry to hear how defeated and hopeless you feel and it may surprise you to know that we agree with giving up hope and accepting defeat in the life you've been living. There's no shame in that. Heroin is a very formidable foe. Where we disagree, and what you seem unwilling or unable to accept right now, is that the life you've been living is very one sided. This world is not just material and is indeed a dichotomy of the good, the beautiful, the true, the hopeful, parts of heaven on earth on one side and evil, ugliness, lies, despair and hell on earth on the other. Heroin clearly falls on the latter side. Please don't give up on the good life/good news side.

Where you find yourself was entirely predictable. What heroin blinds users to is the abject poverty of spirit, body, and emotions that is the end game: death or near death. Although you don't believe it today, you're one of the lucky and blessed ones in that you can still rewrite your ending. Being around someone who is using heroin can be exhausting, so we can only imagine how depleted you must feel. We're asking you to not give up on yourself without first being proactive in giving yourself a chance to change, mature, overcome, and heal. It will take physical, emotional, and spiritual goals and effort. We understand this can look daunting when you are so depleted. But you are not without resources. You are not without accomplishments on which to build. You are not without talents and gifts to further develop. You are not without friends and family who love and support you. You are not without a one-of-a-kind "comfort kitty" who requires a warm lap to sit on and a pair of shoulders to ride.

Life is full of promises. Some good, some bad. We quote God's promises because they're words of beauty, truth and hope.

"The Lord himself goes before you and will be with you; he will never leave you nor forsake you. Do not be afraid; do not be discouraged."
—Deuteronomy 31:8 NIV

Heroin's promise is just the opposite, just as real and just as true.

We say all that to say you've made some seriously bad decisions which have had consequences that are hard to live with. We think we get that. However, hard is not impossible, it's just hard. We're hoping you can get that. Since you gave parts of the past 10 years to decisions that have led you to where you are, we're asking you to consider giving one year to decisions that will prosper and not harm you. You owe it to yourself to at least try. Spend the next year sober and caring for yourself physically, emotionally, and spiritually. Be open to having others come along side you so as not to isolate yourself and to make the shared journey more enjoyable. Sharing the burden also lightens the load. Heroin is efficient in that it just destroys everything in its path as it goes. It doesn't discriminate. Rebuilding a life takes some discriminating, so it will take time. But baby steps and incremental change can be life transforming. A 1% change in direction can change your destination dramatically.

You'll need to answer the lies in your head, probably daily at first, especially first thing in the morning. But since you know they're coming, be ready for them. Hold your ground. You're worth fighting for. Stop dangling over the ledge in Mordor. There are lots of Sam Gamgees with hands extended your way. Muster your last bit of strength and grab hold. Let others and the Lord hold you if you lose your grip.

With all our love,
Mom and Dad

Bobby and Rien

I came face to face with God
And I wrestled for His blessings
I came face to face with the devil
And I kissed him on his left cheek
I was offered life
I was offered death
I was cradled by Mother Earth
But grew into a junk yard
I was born into the American dream
But listened to no one
I was offered life
I was offered death
—Journal entry

———◆◆◆———

This was my last letter written to Bobby when he was in a rehab in September, 2018.

> *Dear Bobby,*
>
> *I just wanted to make a couple of points following our last visit and our last phone conversation.*
>
> 1. *This isn't just about you. It's about you, yes. But it's also about us. I think we've done a pretty good job of hanging with you through addiction for 10 years. What you need to realize is that heroin/drug use has no upside for us. You get high. All we get is stress and fear. This is taking a toll as stress and fear always do eventually and we need a break.*
> 2. *We've continued to give you one more chance, then one more, then another. By any standard worth having, that's insane and enabling and actually reinforces self-destructive behavior. For that we are sorry. We are in this too deep to have a reliable perspective anymore. We need help. You need help.*
> 3. *We are not putting up hoops for you to jump through in order to come home. What we are saying is that we need the house to be drug free. We refuse to live with them.*
> 4. *This is also about trust. Recently it's been alarming how easily you'll lie to us. We know that's part of drug use. You can't very well say "I'm going to Kensington." But we don't want to live there anymore either.*
> 5. *This is also about manipulation which we realize is part of drug use as well. You want to use drugs. But you also*

want to be comfortable. What you need to realize is that we are no longer a recovery option. We've become a continued use option. Helping you in recovery was always our hope and goal, but since this failed, the status quo is no longer tenable. There are other options, and if you stop trying to demagogue us long enough to look around, maybe you'll actually find something useful.

6. This is about where we go from here. We are in this together. However, on your part, there needs to be an intervention, a change agent, a turning off this road onto another, a turn toward the light rather than darkness and hopelessness. Every time you turn to drugs, they welcome you in and then spit you out. No one, ever, anywhere, who's gotten clean, wishes they had stayed in the drug world longer.

7. This is about getting your life back. You say you don't want to be clean, so I'll ask you again to give it a year. Get into serious recovery. Take care of your health. Finish school. Then evaluate whether getting clean was a mistake. Don't make a life-or-death decision until you've actually embraced living. It's certainly not too late. It's never too late.

8. And, finally, as part of a film series at Blue Route Vineyard on Sunday, they talked about the Pixar film, Ratatouille, and asked the question, "What does it mean to be human?" One of the keys is to embrace mercy, grace and love. Drugs can't offer you what they don't have and they don't have mercy, grace or love. The speaker pointed out that we are all writing our stories, that every life has a catastrophe and that every life has the opportunity for redemption and for a happier

ending.[38] *We can always turn the page and start a new chapter. Every life also has supporters and opponents. Often, we are our own worst opponent. We are Gollum, passionately pursuing that which will destroy us. This is enslaving and dysfunctional, not victorious or empowering. This is not to say that life is not painful. This is to say that drugs add to the pain by wrecking us physically, spiritually, emotionally and intellectually. They also wreck our reputations, not only with others, but also in terms of who we think we are.*

9. *You try to idealize and romanticize what you're doing. This is part of the lie you tell yourself to justify continuing such a devastating life style. The reality is Kensington. The reality is the friends you've lost. The reality is pain, heartbreak, destruction, dysfunction, and profound loss from which people never recover. Nothing ideal or romantic about it.*

We love you immensely. There's nothing you can do that would ever change that. We long for a healthy, fulfilling relationship with you. We not only love you, but we like you and want to spend time with you, here and abroad, at family gatherings, sharing books, watching movies, celebrating your graduation, playing tennis, and I could go on...For now, however, we are going to stop our contribution to further harm by accepting that we can't fix the problem or protect you from the consequences of your choices. The last ten years have been trying to teach us this and now we are listening and know it's time. There is no condemnation here. We love you. You have our support and encouragement to become the person you were designed to be. Your creative, curious mind,

---

[38] Andy Crouch Sermons Series, "Ratatouille," Blue Route Vineyard Community Church, September 16, 2018, http://podcast.blueroutevineyard.com/sermon/533-ratatouille.

*compassion, charm, charisma and sense of humor are wonderful
building blocks for your future. Get the help you need to learn to
love a person who is so worth loving, you! Drugs have left you
in physical and emotional pain. Continue down that road and
it will only get worse. Please turn off the drug road and take a
safer one beginning with your current decision to stay longer in
a therapeutic environment. Start a new journey and rely on the
one who is able to "do exceedingly, abundantly above all that we
ask or think!" (Ephesians 3:20 NKJV)*

With all our love,
Mom and Dad

A death from a drug overdose seems so preventable and yet so inevitable at the same time. We've heard people question showing compassion to the addict because he or she is living out the consequences of his or her own actions. I've heard a parent suggest that a good wake up slap should be enough to show the user the error of his or her ways. If it were this simple, the opioid crises wouldn't be a crisis. Often, one use is enough for a drug to begin its takeover and then the battle begins.

Bobby's first major mistake was using drugs in the first place. His second major mistake was not realizing how progressive drug use is. They don't take over all at once. But inevitably they do take over. He wrote the following when he was in rehab for the second time, when he still had some energy, still had some fight. By the time he died, he had neither. He is not the exception for continued drug use. He is the norm. Or he was the norm. The norm is changing because of fentanyl. It has become so pervasive and is so deadly, people often don't survive long enough to have a chance at recovery.

I HATE HEROIN, I hate myself. I hate myself for so many things. The baby in me wants to run away from it all. The coward in me wants to dig a hole so deep no one will find me. But I guess I've been running all along. I've had enough, but I had enough three months ago. I don't know what's different this time. I want my life back! I want to go to college. I want to graduate from college. I want to work in a rewarding field. I want to have money for more than a few hours b/c I blew it up my nose. Most of all, I want to make my parents proud for once, to actually deserve them telling me they are proud. I know I can do it. I know I can't do it without Jesus. I also am scared. I'm scared I'm going to relapse on dope, I'm scared of heroin. I want nothing more than to get past this and move forward with my life. I know I can, and with the help of my parents, God, counselors, meetings, and doctors, I know I will. I could keep writing forever about this now that I'm finally getting it on paper. It hurts. I want to heal; I need to heal. There is no other option. It's life or death. I'm Done. I'm Ready.

He wrote the following in one of his journals. The date is unknown.

Heroin addiction is a war, an inside job. I was hit by two blue bags, hijacked and flown straight into the towers of my heart. One of the worst pains is that I ordered the strike. I planted the charges of thermite which brought down the twin towers of my ego, my ID, my physical wellness, my mental wellness, and then building number seven, my spiritual wellness, came crashing down out of nowhere. I had no idea that my spirituality would be taken as well. Now I am stuck in perpetual war. The troops cannot leave. The insurgency is strong. ISIS has been created. It's called fentanyl.

It's easy to question our decisions as parents, especially when the outcome is not what we were hoping and praying for. I can't help but imagine different scenarios, different choices we could have made, which of course, I envision would have made all the difference. As if it were entirely up to us. Which it never was. I have to accept that we did the best we could trying to keep Bobby from going over the edge while trying not to go over ourselves. It's heartbreaking when our children struggle to this extent in life. We're faced with parenting challenges that we didn't foresee. There is truth behind the family member mantra of rehab centers, "You didn't cause it, you can't control it and you can't cure it."

Those of us with more than one child know how different they can be. The wiring differences between Bobby and his younger sister Hannah were distinct and obvious early on. When learning to walk, Bobby tried to run before he was completely upright. He would cover some distance through sheer will power and was in a hurry to go everywhere. Hannah would get up and stand there for a bit. Just pause. No hurry. And sometimes she decided there wasn't a better place to be and would just sit back down. Bobby always took off. She still knows how to pause to get her bearings or to take a break. Bobby never learned how to pause for anything for very long. The truth was when he had to take a break, it was cause for concern because he found it difficult to stop and focus. Breaks the rest of us look forward to, such as days off, semester breaks or having no plans for the weekend, could spell trouble for him.

Just as with Bobby, we did our best to provide Hannah with everything she needed. She took what we gave her and made the most of it. She's our pride and joy, but she's not our greatest parenting achievement. Bobby is. Hannah was easy. And maybe it's just as true that, given his make-up, Bobby also took what we provided and made the most of it.

In *The Hour of Our Death*, Phillippe Aries says "...the essential characteristic of death as it appears in the *Chanson de Roland* (an epic poem) is that the death, even if sudden or accidental, 'gives advance warning of its arrival.'"[39] We can see three advance warnings of its imminent arrival, all in retrospect. The first warning was with Hannah. When he died, Bobby was in the process of moving into a house in Philly. The Monday of that week he was at our house collecting some things. Hannah came over after work to say hi before he left. He ran up to give her a hug, said that he had been waiting for her and was so glad he got to see her. She was a bit surprised by his level of enthusiasm since he wasn't going far, but it was only in retrospect that she felt it may have

---

[39] Joan Didion, *The Year of Magical Thinking* (New York: Alfred A. Knopf, 2005), 26.

had more meaning than she realized at the time. The second I took note of, but since it involved his cat Rien, I didn't think too much of it. I had texted Bobby something regarding her and he responded with a tearful emoji. Since she was a joy to him, I thought it odd, but then told myself it was because she was staying with us when he moved and he was going to miss her. And the third was one of the last things he said to Bob and me, which was, "You can't say I didn't try." The three of us were in the car at the time. When we dropped him off, Bob and I each got out so we could give him a hug and tell him we loved him because that's what we always did. And Bobby always told us he loved us back. It was three days before he died, the last time we were to see him. When we were on our way home, Bob and I both remarked on his use of the past tense. "You can't say I didn't try." Of course, now, we see it as an omen of what was to come. At the time, it made us uneasy, but we were used to that. In any event, it is true; we can't say he didn't try. We all tried. Helping him get to 29 was challenging, exhausting and worth it.

***

Living is as important as dying.
Do not let words leave you, for once
they do, they transform to smoke.
Living is just as important as dying.
Do not let the words build up inside you,
for, once they do, they turn to a ball of
unpolished stone.
Living is as important as dying.

Do not leave this earth without
Crying out the words; if not, they will
Turn to stone. Because
Living is as important as dying.

Then Narcissus spoke:
We are the moon
We are the sun
We are the stars
Twinkling above.

I'm all alone here, way up on the moon
Did I make a mistake by leaving you all too soon?
—Journal entry

Bobby and Hannah celebrating Hannah's birthday

Bobby Young is in Brenzikofen, **Switzerland.**

August 6, 2018 · 👥

···

I love my @hannahyyoung1 I love this picture of us in a sunflower field in Switzerland. And I loved these green Willy Wonkaish sunglasses I lost somewhere along the road. **#sisterlove** in **#switzerland**

Bobby and Hannah

———◆◆◆———

Athletic Contest

Life becomes much simpler
When one gives up hopes,
dreams, ambitions.
"Why write?" you may then ask.
Because it is the only thing to Reveal the face of Truth in a world full of masks.

Imitation fireplace, the
Great gates of

Nowhere creak open...
For me, *the doors of perception* lead me nowhere.

I know what I know.
I know what my friends know.
Because there's no secrets.
Because there are no secrets.

Will what is energy now, in me,
later burn in some other new
blood?
Will what is buried now,
sprout after the thaw?

Euphoria Again
Two Rights

A miracle of lights,
I have no reason not to indulge
in delight,
except depression eats away, bit/bit
by bit.
To others, seemingly trite.
To me, a life or death fight.
—Redemption Songs

CHAPTER TEN

Rescue

You are not hidden
There's never been a moment
You were forgotten
You are not hopeless
Though you have been broken
Your innocence stolen
I hear you whisper underneath your breath
I hear your SOS
Your SOS
I will send out an army
To find you in the middle of the darkest night
It's true, I will rescue you...
I hear the whisper underneath your breath
I hear you whisper, you have nothing left.
—Lauren Daigle

After the son of dear friends died from an accidental overdose, we talked about how God had rescued him from pain, bondage, and as he called it, "the monkey on my back." On most levels, I believed that God had indeed found him in the middle of the darkest night and had rescued him. But on one nagging level, I didn't find this to be a completely satisfying explanation because of the devastation caused by his loss. Prior to this, I didn't put rescue and death in the same sentence. Rescue to me meant being saved to go on living here. This sense of struggling to reconcile rescue with loss returned when Bobby died.

Bob and I had prayed for years that God would indeed rescue Bobby from his addiction. Bobby was praying for a rescue as well but grew increasingly depleted as he dealt with setbacks. Discouragement and disappointment fueled his depression, which he battled daily. By October 2018, he was sending out a pretty powerful SOS. While hoping for deliverance and relief, he was also looking for an exit where there didn't seem to be one. Then in mid-October, his SOS was heard and he was both found and rescued in the middle of the darkest night.

Still, trying to come to terms with rescue and loss continued until I read *Saving a Life: How We Found Courage When Death Rescued Our Son* by Charles and Janet Morris. This was when I began to accept that death can be a rescue. On the day of her son's death from an overdose, Janet Morris walked down to the beach and asked God to help her deal with her grief and loss of certainty. She randomly opened her Bible looking for an answer and Hebrews 10:17 assured her, "His sins are forgiven and his lawless deeds remembered no more." Those words declared her son Jeff's ultimate and complete well-being. They also declare Bobby's.

The Morrises came to realize that:

> ...a huge tragic mistake, could in reality have been a rescue operation organized by Jesus. God doesn't just come in after the fact and clean up the mess. The Bible represents Him as being in absolute control, sovereign over all things...It made beautiful sense that Jesus would turn his death into a passage out of bondage into freedom.

Charles and Janet's description of their son precisely matched what we could have said about Bobby:

...and yet he always pushed to the edge – the edge of the truth, of what he could safely handle, of what he could get away with...Was he "self-medicating" his anxiety and depression like so many experts told us? Why did he seem so fascinated with anything forbidden, drawn to anything dangerous? Was it because the "normal world" was always out of his comfort zone so he tried to find another place to be? Were they simply choices, sinful choices, he made?

Bob and I often said that one of the main differences between Bobby and Hannah was that she was comfortable in her own skin, while he often was not. Maybe we had that wrong. Maybe it was the "normal world" that was the problem. People want to be in this world with varying degrees of enthusiasm. I struggled with how cavalier, hurried and sometimes indifferent Bobby's approach to life could be. In *Roadrunner: A Film About Anthony Bourdain*, it's said that he was always rushing to get into the scene and then rushing to get out. He was ready to move on to the next thing, even if he had nowhere to go. He's not the only one.

For those of us who have lost children to addiction, we're left trying to reconcile the fact that although they are now free from the devastation and destructive power of drugs, we want them back. Right now, I would take it all back to be able to hug him again, even though his addiction was destroying him. It's convoluted and I don't know how I would have gotten through Bobby's death if not for my friend, Carol Krawiec. When he died, the most frequent beginning to condolences was, "I can't imagine what you're going through." And, for most people, this is true. Carol, however, could not only imagine, she knew. And she handled this knowledge with compassion, understanding, love and skill. Carol's son Dan passed away in 2012 and she's lost two sons, Ben and Tim, since Bobby died. The boys were friends, more like brothers. Carol and I spent many years walking and praying for Hannah and the boys, her five and my one. When we're faced with life's tragedies, we need to find our Carols, the people who know. She wrote the following poem two years after Dan died. Bright light broke through the "darkness of a raging battle" four times in our families. Battles were lost, but God indeed has the victory.

I CHOOSE

Life was forever changed two years ago,
Early on a Saturday morning.
As I sit on the floor of this room
that was once occupied by our son,
I choose not to allow the memory
of the horrific discovery
be my only thought.
I choose to picture this room
as the place of a Holy visitation.
I choose to picture bright light
breaking through the darkness of a raging battle.
I choose to visualize the broken chains
that bound him to addiction
lying on the floor.
I choose to be proud
of the countless battles that our son won
throughout his journey.
I choose to believe
that although the enemy won the battle that day,
God was victorious.
I choose to let the cleansing tears
of a broken heart flow
because I know that Jesus wept.
I choose to lift my hands in worship to my God
and thank Him for the gift of 32 years.
I choose to believe
that although this world is far from good,

my God is good.
I choose peace over anxiety;
acceptance rather than anger;
hope over despair.
I choose to believe that the pain I feel today
Is a reminder that this is not my home.
I choose to rest secure in knowing
that Dan is forever with the Lord. . .
I choose to believe
that even though I am living
In the pain of Saturday,
Sunday is coming
And it will all make sense
When I see Him Face-to-face.
—Carol Krawiec

What follows was written by Carol's son, Ben, following the death of his brother, Dan.

This song is for my hero, mentor, best friend and big brother Dan Krawiec who was tragically taken from us on April 28th 2012 by an accidental heroin overdose the first and last time he relapsed after 6 months in recovery. I hope that addicts in recovery will not take this lesson in vain. This is the train wreck he left behind when he decided to get high one more time. I love you Dan. I hope you can hear this wherever you are.

Kensington
This song is for the dope fiend tryna be clean,
you've been clean and serene for a couple a weeks,
now you're feelin weak and you need a release
so it's back to the streets of Kensington.
This song is for the cowardly who wanna be brave,
but cant cause they crave something hard in their veins,
who stay in NA, countin days on a chain,
or it's back on a train to Kensington.

Another tragic end to a beautiful love story,
all my life I had a brother who adored me.
He's the reason I'm recording and I tour,
but he couldn't stay away from Kensington.
Delaying the inevitable process of healing
pushing back reality with chemical feeling
Choose conflicting views of you staying or leaving,
no comment for those who hover round the grieving.
Am I steppin on your toes thinking it wasn't your time
cause I've been down that road where I was searching for mine
Why'd you get high? What'd you find?
I wish that I could call you up and find the truth you defined
the last 6 months of your meaningful life
and see if there was any meaning on the day that you died.
I wish that I could wipe the bags from under my eyes,
but I've only seen dad cry about a handful of times...

23 years all I wanted was your life
It makes me wanna exit this world like you
when I feel I don't have any more fight left in me
and the best in me will accept defeat and I can rest in peace.
I wish you never loved me, I

wish you never hugged me,
I wish you never taught me what brotherly love means
Then I wouldn't be so fucked up by everything you said to me,
and everything you said I was meant to be, and
everything you taught little Ben to be
has ended in this masterpiece of self-destructive envy and treachery[40]

Tragically, in June of 2021, Ben also lost his life following a long battle with bipolar disorder, compounded by drugs.

His mom Carol and brother Josiah summed him up best.

Carol: For over half of his life, he had to deal with a disease that would throw him into manic episodes of recklessness and depressive episodes of darkness. In spite of all of it and because of all of it, he became this wonderful empathetic, compassionate and loving person. He would be the first one to greet you with a hug and a smile, and the first one to sit with you and comfort you. He loved deeply and was deeply loved...We all need to choose what we believe about God, about life and death. I choose to believe that although Ben's time on earth with us was short, he lives on. Not only in our hearts and memories, but forever.

Josiah: Ben lived and loved with an intensity and passion that most of us will never experience. He had a beautiful and kind soul, but he fought many demons for many years. He was ultimately unable to fight any longer."

I don't think we can overstate how exhausting that fight is. During our last phone call, Ben told me he loved me and "thanks for everything." Benni, I love you too. Thank you for everything. Rest easy. The fight's over.

---

[40] https://soundcloud.com/bkfriendly/kensington.

Ben and Bobby

4 gigs ram

What happens when there is No Exit

Tearing holes in the walls looking for an out

Tumbling down a fire escape which ends in a dangling ladder

Hanging above nowhere

Three stories from the ground

Burn down the building

Save yourself

Realizing efforts made in vain

Realizing all is vanity

Stumbling over cracked checkered sidewalks

Coughing

Through a putrid haze of smoke

Realizing what is left behind

Realizing the rubble of a once great fortress

Lays the foundation for all that is to come.

—Plain Songs

CHAPTER ELEVEN

O Death, Where is Your Victory?

For I am persuaded, that neither death, nor life,
Nor angels, nor principalities, nor powers, nor things present,
Nor things to come,

Nor height, nor depth, nor any other creature,
shall be able to separate us from the love of God,
which is in Christ Jesus our Lord.
—Romans 8:38-39 KJV

Things I Don't Miss:

1. I don't miss routinely checking Messenger for an "Active Now" status for signs of life. If he was online chatting, then all was okay. Long silences could get unnerving. As it turned out though, I actually wasn't that unnerved when Bobby disappeared from social media right before he died. He had just moved into a charming house in South Philly, had a lovely new love interest, a job as a line cook in a nearby restaurant, where he liked the people and they liked him, and finishing school in the spring was a real possibility. Plus, he had mentioned that he was having problems

with his phone and no one was calling me looking for him. That Thursday, I was going to go into Philly after work to help him pick up a futon. But by the time I got home around 3:30, I had a message from him saying that he had been called into work, so don't come. The call into work wasn't true. His last Messenger message to me was "Ty." My second to last to him was trying to reschedule the futon pick up for Friday. Then on Saturday at 11:30 a.m., "Hey Bob, u there?"

2. The other thing I don't miss is being afraid of phone numbers that I didn't recognize because I was afraid the call would be bad news. On the Saturday of the weekend he died, we were on our way home when I noticed I had gotten a call from a number I didn't know with a 215 area code. They left a message. 215 was particularly ominous because it's Philadelphia and that's where Bobby was. So I waited until we got home to listen to the message and made Bob listen with me. It was the call we had been both expecting and dreading for so long. The bullet we had all fought to avoid for ten years had found its mark.

3. Even when Bobby was doing well, we were afraid of another relapse and were often waiting for the other shoe to drop.

Things I Do Miss:

1. Everything else

—◆—

One of the things that surprised me when I first
read the New Testament seriously was
that it talks so much about a dark power in the universe...
Christianity thinks this Dark Power was created
by God, and was good when he was created, and went
wrong. Christianity agrees...this is a universe at war.[41]
—*C.S. Lewis*

—◆—

Bob's message for Bobby's Memorial Service:

Bobby knew he had a loving home. He loved home, and was always comfortable there, maybe a little too comfortable, but his presence has been felt throughout every inch of our home, especially the side porch where he entertained many of his friends. His book shelves are now competing with my book shelves, and for those of you who know me, that is quite a feat.

I'd like to call your attention to the two Scriptures in our memorial program. The first is from 1 John, Chapter 5, verse 13: *I write these things **that you may know** you have eternal life.* **That you may know.** Read First John and count the number of times the word know or knowledge is written, and ask yourself, what does God want us **to know?**

---

[41] C.S. Lewis, *Mere Christianity* (New York: HarperCollins, 2001), 45-46.

The 2nd reading from the letter to the Romans, Chapter 5 vs. 3 mentions rejoicing in our suffering, knowing that suffering produces endurance, endurance produces character, and character produces hope. Bobby knew 1 John 5, and he lived Romans 5. He suffered immensely, almost daily for the past two years. Anxiety, fear, and pain became constant for him. He suffered greatly from depression. It is not a choice for most, and it can be deep, heavy, numbing, and regularly occurring. As a result, he started to self-medicate with prescription and street drugs. He inherited his depressive nature quite naturally. My mom suffered deeply from it. I too have that depressive gene.

Bobby wrote all the time. In a journal, he said:

Death, you exist everywhere
In this cig in my hand, I bring you into me with pulled breaths.
Death, I feared you, so I fought you,
You have yet to win, Death
For I have taken away thy sting
And lay and play, comforted you will one day come,
Keeping you far away
I stare into the sun and I think – Life!

In another journal:

I roll my regrets all up in a ball as one
Lift it high above my head
to be burned by the sun,
Oh my brother it's never an answer to go on the run,
But sit quietly with your pain and it will slowly come undone,
Rejoice! Rejoice! Rejoice!

However, more recently, he no longer feared death, he no

longer fought. Based on a more recent journal entry, he didn't set out to end his life, but he didn't fight to save it.

Because we were so intimately involved in Bobby's struggle, we want to share some of the things we learned. Once a coach, always a coach, so here are my coaching points:

1. Please don't ever give up. *There is always hope.* We would often say those words to Bobby. It's a line by Aragorn from one of our favorite movies, *The Two Towers.* And it's true.

2. Take the time to slow down. Bobby was often anxious and moving. He was intense and his flame burned out much too soon.

3. Don't be afraid to ask for help. It is out there, but you often have to seek it to find it. It doesn't always just show up.

4. Work on your mental health. Bobby fought through some tough times for 10 years. He endured as long as he felt he could.

5. Yet, don't rely just on your feelings, they can be misleading. Bobby did not always feel loved, yet certainly he was immeasurably loved by all of us!

6. Listen carefully to those who love you and to the professionals who can help you.

7. Let's be inspired by Bobby's rejoicing and endurance.

8. The right medications can be found. Keep trying to find the right treatment facility.

9. Be alert. Life's a battle. Be victorious! Be an overcomer, not a victim!

10. Ephesians chapter 6 speaks of preparing yourself for battle. We are given some equipment: A helmet of salvation...wear it. A sword, representing God's Word, use it. A breastplate of righteousness, put it on. Do what's

right. The proper shoes, walk in peace. A shield of faith, carry it, use it as defense. A belt of truth, pursue the Truth!

11. Stay far, far away from all edges. Bobby's last attempt at the edge proved fatal.

12. Don't be reckless. Be resilient, be vigilant, we have an enemy!

For we are not fighting against human beings but against the wicked spiritual forces in the heavenly world, the rulers, authorities, and cosmic powers of this dark age. So put on God's armor now! Then when the evil day comes, you will be able to resist the enemy's attacks (Eph. 6:12-13).

O death where is your victory? Where is your power to hurt? (Where is your power to sting?) "Thanks be to God who gives us the victory through our Lord Jesus Christ" (1 Cor. 15:57 NKJV).

Finally, recognize the differences between disease and sin. Depression and addictions are like cancers. They need medical treatment for healing, not condemnation or guilt. Bobby fought a good fight, lasting at least 12 rounds, yet in the end, worn out, he succumbed, as many do with cancer or other diseases. He couldn't make it to the 13th round, but we can be thankful he fought and fought and fought for years and left us a legacy of love.

Bob, me and Bobby in Colorado

———✦———

Awake from my daydream and stifle a scream
Baking in the midnight moon
I feel as though I left you all
Too soon.
—Journal entry

———✦———

Bobby was loved by his family and he loved everyone in return. He was his Grammy's prince and was forever thankful to his Aunt Eileen for allowing him to move in with her so he could go to the high school in her district. We asked her to say a few words at his Memorial Service.

Memorial Service Remarks by Aunt Eileen, #1 Ridley Mom

Good evening. When I was asked by Bob and Jackie to say a few words, I couldn't, nor did I want to, say no. The only problem is that anyone who knows me knows I have never been a person of few words, but I will try my best.

I was not blessed with having children. I had plenty of the four-footed furry children but never someone who called me mom. Then a 16-year-old boy wanted to go to Ridley High School and, because I lived in Ridley, I offered to have him come live with me. It was one of the best decisions I ever made. To make everything legal, I became Bobby's legal guardian. I couldn't have asked for a better child except for one thing - one bathroom. My idea of getting ready for work is washing my face and running a comb through my hair. Bobby would get up in the morning and it started, the bathroom take over. I wondered what took him so long. I discovered the answer. My bathroom looked like a department in Walmart. I didn't know that many products existed for a young man. I frantically looked for my soap and it was still there, so all was well. Then we got in the car for the ride to school, visor down, mirror-hair. I think he was making sure every hair was standing straight up. Bobby wasn't vain, he just liked to look good, but he sure put me to shame.

Well, it came time for Bobby to leave and I thought my brief motherhood was over, but I was wrong. I was asked to attend his football dinner and was honored. I received a hoodie from Bobby, #1 Ridley mom. Can't explain the feeling I had - Mom. When I was introduced to one of the many girlfriends he had (I apologize if any of you are here) he introduced me as his second mom. I then realized I would always be that to him and I couldn't have been happier or prouder.

The last text I received from him read in part,

"Thank you #1 Ridley mom ever ever. Love you so much. Meow, says Rien."

Then there is Rien, the runt of the litter of 5 kittens I found. Rien was the toughest one to get to drink from a bottle. Bobby and Hannah came to take two of the kittens and Bobby was automatically drawn to the runt, the underdog. I warned him that she would be a handful but that didn't stop him - off she went with her Daddy and an unbreakable bond was born.

That was Bobby - kind, sweet, loving. A lot of people have said that Bobby was thankful to have Jackie and Bob as his parents. He was right, they have helped me in more ways than I can say and I know they did everything in their power to help Bobby.

What I hope Bobby knew is that whether he called us Mom, Dad, sister, Grammy, aunt, uncle, cousin, baby Rien or friend, we were the lucky ones to have him in our lives.

Bobby Henry, go see your grandfather Henry and the others who have gone before you, they are waiting with open arms. It's time to rest now. Though in our hearts you will never be gone, just know we all love you and will miss you.

(Sweetie, every time I hear a Red Hot Chili Peppers song, I will think of you.)

—Aunt Eileen Shelton

Bobby and Aunt Eileen Shelton, "Neese"

Bobby and Grammy, down the shore

For years there was a sealed envelope in Bobby's room that said, "To Me, From Me." I assumed it was written as part of a high school assignment, and as time went on and it was still there, I wondered why he never revisited it. After he died, I opened it and was glad to see how positive it was. He had changed schools for his junior year, felt the new school was a better fit and was happy, "never better." It was gratifying to read that and we are so grateful to his Aunt Eileen for making it possible. Sometimes Bob and I look back and ask ourselves where the missed intervention was. At what juncture could we have prevented him from turning to drugs? Would it have been before or after a semester of "never better"?

At one point, Bobby filled out a values inventory. His top five values were love, spirituality, resilience, adventure and creativity. I don't see him as having given up on any of these. Rather, I believe they were stolen from him because that's what addiction does. It steals and destroys. The theft may be gradual, but without a successful intervention, eventually it's complete. No one is the exception to this. There were times when Bobby believed that he could manage his addiction. Yet, in the end, the darkness descended to the point that he couldn't find his way through. It's possible he could have survived just his recklessness. Or maybe even just the darkness. But the combination of the two overpowered him. We didn't realize their magnitude, nor did we recognize their pervasiveness until we were all in over our heads.

———

One of Bobby's favorite places to spend time, contemplate life and express his creativity was our sunporch. For several years, he had pretty much taken it over with his sketch pads, journals, books, friends and tobacco. It was the only place in the house where he could smoke. It was well lived in and one of the few places where he could unwind.

Bobby and Rien, in the porch

Scene from a Summer Porch

A fireplace in the summer
A most serene scene.
Burning potential, waiting patiently
For a cold soul.

When the sun retreats in his orbit,
Tilted ever slightly, only a few
Celestial
Degrees

I lay a deceased bouquet of flowers,
A gift waiting to be burned open.
Alive again.

Potential energy
Potential energy
Potential energy

Your life is a poem.
Your life is *this*.
Write it.
Live with passion.

Potential energy
Potential energy
Kinetic
The moon behind her clouds
She sits boastful and proud
The sun shining his rays
Smiling
Knowing he will be here until the end of days.

I bow my head knowing
That gods meet the same fate as man.

Potential energy
Potential

Energy
Kinetic
—Siren Songs

Bobby and baby Rien

Wilmington Wharf Rats
have now become my pets
Rien clings to my shoulder for she is a cat
Found lost and abandoned
She brings me back to life
This creature, sucking from the bottle
I am its father
I will let you outside
I will let you be free
Just beef up first baby
This is Chester, and a dark cat
is lurking in the alley, spraying.
Take back our yard, my beautiful Wilmington wharf rat.
—Journal entry

Chapter Twelve

Only the Soul is Invincible

Dirge Without Music by Edna St. Vincent Millay

I am not resigned to the shutting away of
loving hearts in the hard ground.
So it is, and so it will be, for so it has been, time out of mind:
Into the darkness they go, the wise and the lovely. Crowned
With lilies and with laurel they go; but I am not resigned.

Lovers and thinkers, into the earth with you.
Be one with the dull, the indiscriminate dust.
A fragment of what you felt, of what you knew,
A formula, a phrase remains, —but the best is lost.

The answers quick and keen, the honest look, the laughter, the love, —
They are gone. They are gone to feed the roses. Elegant and curled
Is the blossom. Fragrant is the blossom. I know. But I do not approve.
More precious was the light in your eyes than all the roses in the world.

Down, down, down into the darkness of the grave
Gently they go, the beautiful, the tender, the kind;
Quietly they go, the intelligent, the witty, the brave.
I know. But I do not approve. And I am not resigned.

In *Death: The Final Stage of Growth*, Elisabeth Kubler-Ross writes that one of the hardest deaths to accept is that of a child. "It's a rude reminder that death follows no predictable timetable, but chooses its own timing and place. Painful though this experience is, it can also be an impetus to growth for those who accept the challenge."[42]

Kubler-Ross provides two extremes for coping with the death of someone we love, living in grief and remorse versus acceptance. She says that to move out of grief we must face and work through our feelings so we can emerge with an acceptance of death and a commitment to living on the other side.[43] Working through grief and emerging on the other side can be a long road and it's quite possible to linger or backtrack along the way. How long we stay on the road is as individual as we are. I like her use of the word emerge. In order to move forward again, we are forced to move out of life as we knew it and work through our grief. Only then can we come into view and emerge on the other side. However, when it comes to acceptance of death, I'm in agreement with poet Edna St Vincent Millay. "I am not resigned and I do not approve." And I can accept that, yet still have a commitment to living. Life is full of paradoxes. I recently read the following quote regarding how Jesus so often spoke paradoxically, "It would be nearer the truth to say that it is life itself which is paradoxical and that the sayings of Jesus are simply a recognition of that fact."[44] Bobby's life and death also seem to confirm this. In some ways he endured, and, in others, he surrendered.

There are a lot of different ways to work through grief. Time helps. Kindness helps. I like to be alone, but I'm sure this isn't true for everyone. Especially during the first year, I gave myself a lot of time to try to come to

---

[42] Elisabeth Kubler-Ross, *Death: The Final Stage of Growth* (Upper Saddle River NJ: Prentice Hall, 1975).
[43] Kubler-Ross, *Death: The Final Stage of Growth*.
[44] Sir Tom Taylor in University of Edinburgh Journal, vol. xvi, no 2 (1952), p. 96.

terms with where we now were and to create a space I could function in. Even now, I can't always find that space, but over time it does become easier. Bobby died in mid-October. By the time we could breathe again, the holidays were upon us. We got through them and then I disconnected as much as possible for the month of January. In every way, January is the perfect month to do this because it's cold and dark and climbing into bed at 9:00 doesn't feel all that extreme. The second January, I took this a step further and went away for a couple of days by myself. I went "down the shore" as we say in Philly. The beach was delightfully deserted and I took long walks and read and slept and thought and wrote.

People often initiate rituals to help them deal with grief as well as to try to stay connected to the people they love who have passed away. In *Care of the Soul*, psychotherapist and former monk Thomas Moore says that "Ritual maintains the world's holiness." No matter how simple, they serve our souls and enrich our lives.[45] For those of us now connected to death in a profound, daily, and unrelenting way, establishing rituals that feed our souls may maintain the world's holiness on a cosmic level, but they help preserve our sanity on a personal one. "They are unique opportunities for communication, ventilation, and appropriate acting out."[46] I plan to make tuning out for January one of mine. I'm not referring to the more public rituals associated with mourning such as wearing black, sitting Shiva or Mass Cards, although important, but am thinking on a more personal level. "No matter how simple."[47]

I don't put much emphasis on dates or counting time other than his birthday and the date he died. In between those two dates, August 1st, 1989 and October 19th, 2018 was the gift of Bobby's life here with us. I'll always mark both of those days. However, from the time he left us until we see him again, the loss is the same. He's equally not here on day one, as on day 100, as on day 1000.

---

[45] Thomas Moore, *Care of the Soul* (New York: Harper Perennial, 1994), 226.
[46] Therese A. Rando, PH.D., How To Go On Living When Someone You Love Dies: A Book of Hope, Understanding, and Comfort (New York: Bantam Books, 1991), 261.
[47] Thomas Moore, *Care of the Soul,* 226.

That said, even though the passing days don't lessen the feeling of separation for me, they do put distance between me and constant grief. One day I heard myself talking to our dog in that voice that's reserved for babies and our pets. It had been 15 months since I'd heard that rather high-pitched, happy voice asking the dog, "Who's the Tweedles?" She didn't answer nor did she let on whether or not she was happy to have that voice back.

In *Composing a Life*, written in 1990, Mary Catherine Bateson addresses the changing roles and increased opportunities for women in the preceding 20 or so years. What she said at that time resonates with my current situation as well, 30 years later. She talks about life as an improvisatory art, "about the ways we combine familiar and unfamiliar components in response to new situations." Bateson adds this sometimes leads to "desperate improvisation . . . trying to make something coherent from conflicting elements to fit rapidly changing settings."[48]

There are many situations and events in life that lead us to "desperate improvisation." My hope is that by recognizing this and by accepting that I need "to make something coherent from conflicting elements" will, over time, make the improvisation less desperate and lead to what Bateson calls a "path of preference."[49] My first-choice path of preference is no longer in play, but I can, with God's help, forge a new one.

[48] Mary Catherine Bateson, *Composing a Life* (New York: Grove Press, 2001), 3
[49] Mary Catherine Bateson, *Composing a Life*, 4

Bobby, me and Grammy

"You must take care to light the matches one at a time. If a powerful emotion should ignite them all at once, they would produce a splendor so dazzling that it would illuminate far beyond what we can normally see; and then a brilliant tunnel would appear before our eyes, revealing the path we forgot the moment we were born, and summoning us to regain the divine origins we had lost. The soul ever longs to return to the place from which it came, leaving the body lifeless."
—Laura Esquivel

When I read this quote in *Like Water for Chocolate*, I wondered if some souls long to return to the place from which they came more intensely than others. Over time, Bobby became increasingly detached and once told us that he only wanted to live so he didn't hurt us. I found this hard to comprehend, especially in light of how much people manage to cope with and overcome: illness, accidents, injury, depression, loss. We have so many examples of those who have triumphed over adversity and have gone on to lead meaningful lives. Bobby and many who have come before him, and many who will come after, struggle with meaning itself. And, because of this, they also struggle to endure. My natural inclination is to believe that, if faced with a devastating illness or injury, I would fight to survive. I believe I would look for a way to stay here. Life had a way of wounding Bobby's soul, so he was looking for a way out.

In "My Only True Friend," musician Gregg Allman anticipated his death when he said he hoped others would be "haunted by the music" of his soul after he died.[50] I'm not entirely sure what he meant by this, but I do think that the music of one's soul is a beautiful way to describe what we're left with. The drugs, pills, depression, anxiety and pain are no longer here to cloud our view of Bobby, or his view of himself, and we're left with the music in his soul. It's not just a memory. It's what lives on. Maybe Allman realized this because he was so close to his own death when he wrote these words. They're evocative and I am haunted, not because I didn't hear the music in Bobby's soul when he was here, but because, increasingly, he didn't.

---

[50] officialgreggallman, "My Only True Friend (Lyric Video) | Gregg Allman - Southern Blood," YouTube (YouTube, August 9, 2017), https://www.youtube.com/watch?v=EVFoMG9PHh4.

Only the spirit
Only the soul
Is invincible
—Journal entry

the fly
falls through the open window
the wind funnels through
a wing cripples
pinch him between my fingers
let him blow back along the interstate
was he meant to die on my lap?
or did this car interior interrupt natural causes?
my head is a cage
my mind is locked away
when will my soul blow through a window
to a welcoming lap.
—Plain Songs

CHAPTER THIRTEEN

What Becomes of One
With a Broken Compass?

*There are gaps in the mesh of the everyday world, and
sometimes they open up and you fall through them into
somewhere else. Somewhere Else runs at a different pace to the
here and now, where everyone else carries on.... Somewhere
Else exists at a delay, so that you can't quite keep pace.*
—Katherine May

The above quote was taken from a book by Katherine May called *Wintering: The Power of Rest and Retreat in Difficult Times*. She describes wintering as the fallow times, the difficult, and sometimes unbearable times that are "usually involuntary, lonely, and deeply painful."[51] May says, "We may never choose to winter, but we can choose *how*."[52] It's not easy to respond to an outcome we didn't choose, don't want and would do anything in our power to change. But if we allow them, even the dark days and an acceptance of sadness and retreat can become transformative.

Our last contact with Bobby is a moment in time. It's natural to want to hold onto as much of that moment as we can so we don't completely

---

[51] Katherine May, *Wintering* (New York: Riverhead Books 2020) 11
[52] Katherine May, *Wintering*, 13

lose touch. One of the last memories I have of Bobby is when we were waiting for him to finish his shift at The Barcelona Wine Bar in Philly. We were being taken very good care of by the staff and could see back into the kitchen where he was busy chopping stuff. He looked good. I want to bring Bobby and our memories forward in a way that's not unhealthy or morbid. I'm happy to have voicemail messages, "Hey Mommy...it's me." I have cards and letters telling me he loved me, but hearing him say it on the old messages is priceless. I regret there won't be more but I'm thankful to have the ones I do. I still have the text messages telling me that "I'm da man." Whenever I would do something for him, I would text "who's da man?" He never once failed to humor me by assuring me that indeed I was. While going through his things I was glad that he didn't throw anything away because I came across an old fill-in-the-blank school assignment that lists me as his favorite relative. I don't remember ever seeing it before and wish I knew how old he was when he wrote it. At the time, I was "an amazing and wonderful person," so it's a keeper just in case anybody around me should doubt this. I have it in writing. On the same assignment, under "If I could do anything for a year, I would..." he wrote, "Go to Heaven."

Remembrances are important. I'm typing this at our friend's house near the beach and most rooms have some representation of an anchor, which is a symbol of safety, security and hope. Our friends, Fran and Carol, lost their son who had a tattoo of an anchor and to be reminded of him as I stay here is as it should be. It's a comforting remembrance of what an anchor symbolized to Dan.

> *Which hope we have as an anchor of the soul, both sure and*
> *steadfast, and which enters into that within the veil.*
> *—Hebrews 6:19 KJV*

I originally started writing this both as a means to cope and to commemorate Bobby. Going through the things he wrote to include them here keeps him close and keeps him involved. In the days and weeks following his death my head was crammed with so many thoughts that were hard to keep straight, so writing them down was therapeutic. At the time, I had an early morning, hour-long commute, and as I drove, I would watch the sun come up and the starlings swarm and this book started to take shape. Then, as Bob or I would mention that I was writing a book and incorporating things Bobby wrote, there was interest and encouragement from family and friends, so that was one of the things that kept me going.

Another thing that kept me going was putting some order to the things Bobby left behind. Addiction is always messy and often chaotic. And this messiness and chaos spills over onto everything and everyone it comes into contact with. We went through his belongings bit by bit; there was no deadline, no hurry. His things offered proof that a life was being lived. Shirts, shoes, hats, books, notes, letters, a passport, transcripts, ticket stubs, pay stubs, pictures, a guitar, vitamins, matcha tea. All this stuff just left behind. Along with his cat. Did she forget him? Or did she get tired of waiting for him to come back? We put some things aside for friends, some went back on the shelf to decide another day, and some we were ready to toss or donate. We all kept some clothes, as did his friends, but there are still some things in his drawers and his bookcases are full. Not long ago, I was wearing a jersey that's too big but nonetheless perfect for those early spring days when you think you may have turned off the heat too soon, and I was wondering where I got it. Then, not too long after, I was looking through some pictures and there it was on Bobby. Sometimes we stumble into memories.

But the hard truth is that no matter how much I organize his words and his things, or wrap myself in his clothes, his death will never be manageable. Most of life is like when we're singing along to a familiar song and there's a line or two that we're not quite sure of, so we make up some words that fit and soldier on. They may not be what was originally intended, and sometimes don't even make sense, but they let us keep going. My favorite twisted lyric is courtesy of my sister Eileen who swapped "A girl with kaleidoscope eyes" with "A girl with colitis goes by" in "Lucy in the Sky with Diamonds."[53] It works and a lot of life is like this. We can take what comes along and find a way to make it fit, so we can carry on. But not everything is like this. Not everything fits. Sometimes, life is more like the line in "Across the Universe," another Beatles' song, for which I tried to come up with words that fit for 50 years. Then one day my underperforming curiosity got the better of me and I looked it up. It's Sanskrit. English was never going to fit. Now when I hear it, it's so obviously not English that I don't know how I thought it was for so long. It didn't occur to me that I had the wrong reference point. With Bobby, it was as if I was encouraging and trying to help him in English and he was saying "You can't understand Mom. My life is Sanskrit. You have the wrong reference point." In many ways, his death is Sanskrit too. This side of heaven, I don't expect I'm ever going to understand it. When exactly did the smiling, active child in the pictures derail? And why? Did he betray his brain? Or did his brain betray him? Bobby asked a similar question in a poem, "Which came first? The addict or the patient?"

<hr/>

Searching for the roots
The fruits fall all around
Which came first?
The addict or the patient
A doctor's death sentence
A priest's condemnation
The hills are alive with the sound of simple minds

[53] "The Beatles - Lucy in the Sky with Diamonds See," Genius, accessed August 15, 2020, https://genius.com/The-beatles-lucy-in-the-sky-with-diamonds-lyrics.

The toils of labor
Reap what is sown
unmarked graves
unmask the corruption
coursing through the dead blood of masked politicians

Neurons firing and frying between the temples
A static wave of indignity
Just show me how to be free
Or pulsate with me toward distant nebulae

Which came first?
Man's fall or man's salvation

—Plain Songs

In another one of his poems, Bobby asked, "What becomes of one with a broken compass?"

U-turn. Leave the unholy otherworldly siege of temptations.
Judas Iscariot ascending as Icarus only to realize inevitably dust settles.
What becomes of one with a broken compass?

If you're reading this, and are struggling with addiction, if your compass too is broken, it's not too late to change. It's not too late to get a new compass. It's never too late to find the help you need. If you think you are too far into your addiction to change, or think you've burned too many bridges, go to *The Addicts Diary* on Facebook. You'll see it's not just me, and the people who love you, saying this. It's people who are celebrating their sobriety and encouraging you that if they can get clean, and stay clean, you can too. These are people who have been where you are. They share your reference point. They understand the Sanskrit.

The following was posted on *The Addicts Diary* by a mom on the one-year anniversary of her son's death. He too lost a 10-year battle with addiction. It's so well written and true that, with her permission, I want to share it here as well.

Suzanne DeCosta
August 26 at 7:41 AM
Michael DeCosta

A year ago yesterday this box was an empty amazon delivery box waiting for recycle. A year ago today we filled it with your favorite shoes and clothes you had recently bought in your next attempt to start fresh, start over. We filled it with some cherished new and cherished lifetime memory items, in hopes that we could send you off surrounded by all the things, and with all the people that you loved. You were loved by all that knew you, but somehow didn't love yourself. A ten-year battle with addiction was lost. You fought long and hard. Your courage to keep trying is something we will always be proud of and grateful for. We are thankful that you did enjoy many lengthy periods of success and recovery. During those beautiful periods of recovery, we would see the light return to your eyes, the smile return to your face and your amazing sense of humor entertain everyone around you. Best of all those periods of recovery allowed you to look your parents in the eye, and yourself in the mirror with a sense of pride and dignity.

Things I've learned in the last ten years:

Addiction is a disease not a disgrace.

Why you started and why you can't stop are two different things.

It's a medical condition masquerading as a personal choice.

It's physical, spiritual, and mental.

It's deceptive and sneaks up on you.

It's progressive, when you can stop you won't want to, when you want to stop you won't be able to.

It's a chronic, long-lasting condition that can't be cured, but can be successfully treated.

Addiction does what it takes to survive, and left untreated - is deadly

Things I hope you will learn if you still struggle:

Sobriety is not a sad consequence, it's a proud choice.

That all of your mistakes can serve as purpose, instead of shame.

That you can't heal if you keep pretending you are not hurt.

That no program is perfect and if you are going to recover, you have to take with you what works and leave the rest behind.

If there are pieces of your past weighing you down, that you decide it's time to leave them behind.

That you find the answer to what it is you believe about yourself keeping you from your future.

That you realize, if you are still breathing you can decide that today starts a do-over. Michael won't get a do-over.

If I had a do-over, I would have given one last hug. And spoken many less harsh words. If I had a do-over I would have pleaded with him to give treatment one more try, and even if he still walked out that door that day, I would have reminded him that I loved him, just in case he didn't know. Spent most of yesterday feeling paralyzed and at a loss for words. These anniversary dates really suck. I miss you Michael, your dad misses you, your sisters miss you, and Oliver misses you 🐾 I hope your struggle is over, and I pray I will see you again.

———◆◆———

Opioid deaths have been rising in the US from 21,088 in 2010 to 47,600 in 2017 to 49,860 in 2019. Bobby was one of 46,802 in 2018.[54] The numbers are overwhelming and continuing to rise. For information and direction, there's a wealth of information regarding substance abuse and behavioral health on the SAMHSA.gov web site.

---

[54] www.drugabuse.gov

CHAPTER FOURTEEN

Could Never Be Heaven

The following three letters were written by me, Bob and Hannah, in that order.

> *Dear Bobby,*
>
> *It's now September of 2021. How we're doing still depends on when you ask us. I'm somewhere between "The greatest tribute to the dead is not grief but gratitude" and "What restraint or limit should there be to grief for one so dear?" In other words, I'm somewhere between Thornton Wilder and the Roman poet Horace. Next month will be three years since we lost you. I first started writing to organize my thoughts and the things you wrote. Then it was to self-publish it to share with family and friends. Now my goal is simply to finish what I have to say by one of my arbitrary deadlines, that I've yet to adhere to, and then decide what to do next.*
>
> *Some good things happened in the first year after we lost you. The Philly Fringe production on addiction was performed several times in September 2019 and included your story. We went to see it twice. It was well done and, of course, emotional for us. One of the nicest things about the whole production was the people involved with it. We are happy to have met them and I hope our paths cross again. A really nice gesture was that they called the show Siren Songs to honor you and your poetry.*
>
> *Something else that was totally unexpected and that we are so thankful for is that Dr. Parker and Dr. Lieberman established*

a prize in your honor at Widener University to be given each spring to a senior arts student who "displays a passion for and belief in the power of art." The first Robert Young Memorial Prize in the Power of Art was awarded to a student who was described as being a kindred spirit of yours. Dad and I attended the Humanities Awards Ceremony via Zoom. Zoom and the Covid 19 pandemic is a whole other story, a whole other book. The graduating senior who received the prize spoke and we could clearly see why he was chosen. Drs. Parker and Lieberman wanted something positive that would link your memory with a field you loved and that would show how much you meant to them. To "want something positive to come from Bobby's passing... to keep him in our hearts and minds" speaks volumes about the type of people they are. And the type of person you were.

Hannah is doing well, both personally and professionally, and moved out of the back house with her friend Emily, Ash the cat, and Emily's dog, Ollie. They signed a lease for a house in Philly that's perfect for them. Even Ash, who spent nearly every waking minute plotting how to escape when he was out back, has settled in and is quite content. So far, they all love it. Hannah used your ticket to Circa Survive and went with Ben and Bridget and one of her friends. Ferry used your ticket to mewithoutYou and went with Rossi.

Many of your friends are still, or have become, our friends. We keep in close touch with Ferry. We'll occasionally meet him for dinner and he'll often stop in when he's in the area. Ryan moved to Arizona. We went to his going away party and he thanked us for being there to "represent you." Senjen wrote to ask if I still had the orange hat, which I did, so now it's back in Wyoming with him. We continue to celebrate your birthday with your friends.

But sad things have happened as well since we lost you. Our hearts were broken again in May of 2019 when Tim lost his battle with depression and addiction. Only seven months after you. I often thought you and Tim shared some similarities, especially in how intense you both were in your approach to life. He had just spent Memorial Day with his family, but also like you, he sometimes found it difficult to cope when alone. Ben (his brother) found him the next day. Following his death, a lot of people commented on how much Tim had meant to them and how supportive he had been, especially in helping them to navigate recovery. This was true for us too.

Then in June we lost Ben. We are reeling. I can't even think about him yet. It's not just that I can't accept that there will never be another random call saying he's in Delco and will stop by. Or that I won't be getting another leather jacket bear hug. But it's also that he took all of his memories of you with him. I miss him and I miss his connection to you. He got caught in a downward spiral that he wasn't able to overcome. He did try. He recently shared a song he wrote "with you," using words from one of your poems and was excited at the prospect of recording it. But then depression and suicidal thoughts intervened. We returned to the cemetery where we said good-bye to Tim, just two years earlier, for Ben's graveside service. Both Carol and Fran (Ben's parents) spoke with wisdom and comfort in the midst of their profound grief. They and their family are among the most remarkable, caring people we know. Dan, Tim and Ben must be so proud of them.

Our losses haven't been limited to people. Rien is gone too. She was wonderful and her normal self until this past March when we were blindsided by a diagnosis of feline leukemia. Since she's the third in her litter of five to die from this, it's clear their mom was a carrier. Riennie put up a good fight, but we knew when it was time to say good-bye. Our love for her connected us to you which makes it exceptionally hard. She was so cute, loving and full of personality, we miss her terribly. I know how much you loved her. And how much she loved you. She went from runt to royalty and no cat ever deserved it more.

So, time goes on, as it always does when someone leaves this life. But, of course, for those left behind, life is never the same. You are missed and always will be. As hard as that is for us, it's only right. You can't love someone as much as we love you and not be forever changed by having known you. You enriched our lives beyond measure and for that we will be forever grateful. Thank you from the bottom of our hearts for being ours. Rest in peace, sweet boy, rest in peace.

Love, Mom

Dear Bob,

Since we lost you, I've struggled daily with why. Was it a broken compass? Was it faulty brain circuitry or a chemical imbalance that fostered depression? Was it a negative, glass half empty mental pre-disposition that created a poor self-image and a desire to numb the pain, and in the end, self-destruct? Was it a heart-breaking combination of the above? I'm still not sure, but very recently found something that's been beneficial in helping me to begin to understand. You know without me telling you that it was in a book. This one is called The Healing of Damaged Emotions by David Seamands. In it Seamands compares the rings in the bark of a tree to the rings or protective layers of our psyches.

> ...the naturalists can show you a cross section of a great tree they have cut, and point out that the rings of the tree reveal the developmental history, year by year...
> And that's the way it is with us. Just a few minutes beneath the protective bark, the concealing, protective mask are the recorded rings of our lives. These are scars...

painful hurts...(physical and mental infirmities) causing all kinds of interpersonal difficulties...And these scars are not touched by conversion and sanctifying grace, or by the ordinary benefits of prayer...

It is necessary that we understand this, first of all, so that we can compassionately live with ourselves...We also need to understand this in order to not judge other people too harshly, but to have patience with their confusing and contradictory behavior...They are people, like you and me, with hurts and scars and wrong programming that interfere with their present behavior."

I think the insight that it's important to understand this "so that we can compassionately live with ourselves" may provide some answers to "Why?" Not being compassionate with ourselves leads to problems, not just in being able to live in harmony with ourselves, but also in how we relate to the world around us. I know this was an area where you struggled and that led to decisions that made you feel even less compassionate toward yourself. The part of you that would tell you the truth became increasingly harder to reach. I think it's important for you to know that we never lost sight of who you really are, the beautiful, kind, intelligent, opinionated, funny, loving you. The addiction stunted you from, as I so often encouraged you, "growing in the grace and knowledge of our Lord and Savior, Jesus Christ." (2 Peter 3:18). We miss you; we'll never stop loving you, and are looking forward to seeing and being with you again someday!

Love, Dad

Dear Bobby,

Discovering new music, reading a new book, or traveling to new places are always a little bit less exciting now because I can't share them with you. So much of who I am today is because of you. When I was 6, my favorite thing to do was sit and watch you play video games just so I could hang out with you. When I was 13, I started listening to alternative/indy music, just to impress you and get your "cool little sister" stamp of approval. When I was 19, I wanted to travel to places you went, even if it meant going halfway across the globe. Whether I recognized it or not, I was always chasing after you trying to keep up.

While there was so much I looked up to you for, our relationship was complicated and there was also a lot of you that I didn't understand. Over the years I built up resentment and anger watching you destroy your body and hurting our family. I simply didn't understand. In my naivety, I didn't understand why you couldn't just put the drugs down permanently, seek help, be happy… were we not worth it? I felt helpless and looked to you as the only person who had the power to change the nightmare our family was living in. Because of that, I know I started to push you away in an effort to protect myself. I'm sorry for not always seeing or understanding you, for not approaching you with more grace and forgiveness. I understand now. You weren't selfish or weak, you were so incredibly strong and resilient. You faced a darkness and reality I can't even comprehend and yet you still filled your life with so much joy and accomplishment. You clung to your passions and love for people even when you were at your lowest points. You tried your absolute best to show up for me and be a reliable big brother, even when you often couldn't show up for yourself. You fought so hard for so long and I'm so proud of you now for that.

Now, at 27, I'm still trying to follow in your footsteps and make you proud. Your ability to fill a room and make anyone in it feel seen and cared for, your sense of humor, your love of the arts, your tenacity for life and adventurous spirit – I'll never be able to do you justice but I'll spend my life trying.

While so much of what I do is bittersweet because I can't share it with you or tell you about it, it's much more meaningful. I do it for us now. I do it for you. And I can't wait to catch you up in heaven!

Love, Hannah

These letters had been the end of the book for some time, but I had an encounter that I want to include and it belongs here, at the end. I haven't believed in the existence of a purely material world for a long time. I believe that Heaven is a real place and that angels walk among us and that they are messengers, which is what their name means. I believe that sometimes their message changes the world and sometimes it simply comforts a heart. Finding feathers and coins and seeing cardinals are all viewed as signs that angels are near, providing a connection to someone who has died. I do understand how spotting any of these can easily be seen as simply random or coincidental and not as a sign of anything supernatural. Nevertheless, I'm in the group of coin and feather finders and cardinal watchers. Finding feathers has more meaning for me than coins because, when I was a little girl, I'd find feathers to give to my dad who would put them in his shirt pocket to "show to all the men at work." So, I have a history with them. Once Bob and I were looking for a particular entrance to a beach that had significance for Bobby, but weren't sure we'd found the right place. It was one of those windy days when the sand blows up in your face, but I muttered anyway, "Bobby let us know if this is the right spot." I glanced over and there was a feather stuck in the grass in the dunes. Then, for good measure, I noticed something white flutter on the sand. At first, I ignored it because it was too windy for a feather to just flutter and not be carried away, but on second glance, it was indeed another one. To me, they weren't random. These are small things, but I love it when they happen anyway. I believe in signs. I believe, as Martha Whitmore Hickman says in *Healing After Loss,* that "the creation continues to embrace us and all those whom we love. We are still somehow bound together in a giant conspiracy of love, mutual care, and ongoing life. As we are not lost to creation, we are not lost to one another."[55]

But I'd never had an actual "encounter" like people sometimes do with loved ones they've lost. These meetings are often described as being in dreams that are so real, they have a palpable presence. But I can now say that I've had one. It was early morning and I was asleep, but it didn't feel like a dream in the normal sense. It was so profound that after I woke up, I typed up what happened before I did anything else so I'd get it right. And all that day, I had a disorienting sense of not fitting in with time. What felt like only a 10- or 15-minute time lapse would actually be an hour. Like I was out of synch. I know for certain that this dream is not like anything I've ever experienced before. I've had several dreams with Bobby in them since he died. They made me sad and made me miss him more, but didn't feel as if they had any deeper meaning. This one does.

Here's the dream:

I was upstairs in our house, in the hall, Bobby came up and I followed him into the bathroom. He looked great, healthy, calm, not so much happy as very sure of himself, at peace. His hair was short, his clothes were light, summery. I recognized the shirt. The best way I can describe it is everything about him looked clean and light, but real. I just wanted to touch and hug him to make sure he was real, which I did. And he told me he was real. I was, of course, confused and asked him where he'd been for 2 years. He gestured vaguely and said "over there." It was almost as if he could have been a few blocks away, but I somehow knew it wasn't a place I could get to or where I could visit him. He also said he was with other people and that they were doing good things. It was clear he was going back. I then briefly stepped out of the room and when I went back in, Bob was sitting on the windowsill and Bobby was on the floor, grey, eyes back in his head like an overdose. He was wearing different clothes than he had been wearing a minute before

---

[55] Martha Whitmore Hickman, *Healing After Loss: Daily Meditations for Working Through* Grief (New York: Harper Collins, 1994).

and his hair was longer. The rug on the floor wasn't the one we have now, it was an old one. Bob and I both just looked at him, neither of us tried to help. I wondered how he could have ended up in that condition so quickly. Then, the first Bobby stood up away from the body on the floor. His hair was short again, he was wearing the same summer clothes, and he was once more clear-eyed, confident and sure of himself. He told us that that experience on the floor led to the most wonderful experience he could ever have. At first, both Bob and I misunderstood and thought he was talking about the drug high being wonderful and I felt momentarily completely disheartened. But that wasn't what he meant. Once we realized that he was referring to his current state as being the most wonderful experience he could ever have, the encounter was instantly over. It felt like more of a business trip than a social call. Bobby is where he wants to be, doing something he wants to do. And although he may continue to be around us (after all, he said he was just "over there") I don't sense he'll be back in the same way. For now, I believe we know what he wanted us to know and he trusts us enough to understand.

And yet, as angles in some brighter dreams
Call to the soul when man doth sleep:
So some strange thoughts transcend our wonted themes,
And into glory peep.[56]

And that's how I feel. That I into glory peeped.

⇒◆⇐

Project A World
Shall I Project A World,
Scatter full the sky with constellations

---

[56] Henry Vaughan, *Silex Scintillans* (1650).

and create my own private universe?
The dead are never gone,
but still ever persist,
in the bread we eat
and
the wine we drink.
Long ago our names were written.
Long ago our names were etched.
Do you think for one moment
this was all an accident?
Or do you doubt that any of
this is real?
Or do you feel
////that all this is a reflection in the water pond
a cast stone disturbing all reality as it ripples outward////
—Siren Songs

Hofbrauhaus, Munich

ADDITIONAL POEMS

DEUS EX

What do I hold in my hands?
my future
or does the future
float far above
a grey cloud
ready to burst
or
sliding aside to reveal the sun
What do I hold in my hands?
My past has already slipped through.

GRAPES GROW NOW IN POMPEI

Pompei the lost city
Still had gratitude and looked really pretty,
Leave the corpses buried what a pity
what a pity
Dig deeper Dig deeper
Move past the ugly corpses and ash
Dig deep enough to find the beauty
What you find deep down there by digging and digging
We find what we are looking for
Your beauty was always there
Grapes grow now in Pompei

Six Feet Under

All my heroes are dead

Dylan Thomas: take me by the hand lead me under skies of milkwood, shelter me

from the ever-approaching darkness of the

Cold

Bitter

Night

Henry Miller: show me the guise and charm to winning a woman

Fyodor Dostoevsky: sit me down, educate me on not being the idiot

Bukowski: take me to the races, help me free the bluebird in my heart

Camus: save me from this strange plague

Caligula is at the door demanding my firstborn.

So, Salley

where does the red fern grow?
Come on Doc, just give me something
Did I drive out here for nothing
Is it back to the unabashed unforgiving streets
For me
You go home to a family and watch Glee
While I shaking shivering search for a fleeting relief
There is no relief from one's own mind
You pay a fee you can't see
Every time you flee further down that wicked road
Just know,
There is no guarantee of safe passage home
Oh.
When will I You Everyone we know
Ever.
Learn.

Dear Nietzsche,
If God is love
Then when God died
Did love survive
If God is love
And love is real
The dead are dancing with the dead

STILL LIFE WITH WOODPECKER: ODE TO TOM ROBBINS

Pondering,
Who knows the secret,
Of how to make love remain?
Painting, stroke after brush stroke of
Still life with pyramids.
Those ancient symbols of death and rebirth,
Of love and the infinite.
Pondering,
What is the secret of the moon,
What does she hide from the mortals below?
Floating forever circling above.
I know she hides a hidden purpose.
Although, when I point, reaching my finger up towards her above,
She seems just out of reach.

Wandering,
Inside a pack of Camel cigarettes,
Searching for oasis in the dry and solar charred landscape.
Smoking is our own little private communion with fire.
Who knows how to make love stay?
What is the purpose of the moon?
These are the secrets I inquire of the fire gods,
As I wander and wonder,
Inside a pack of Camel cigarettes.
Smoking is our own little private communion with fire.

ART ANGELS

When dead men tell no tales,
My poetry still spouts from the grave,
to the tune of taps, a melody over the air,
signaling I shan't be saved.
She drops me off at the intersection of last year and tomorrow.
I look ahead with anticipation and
behind with sorrow.
Why do I cry out in distress?
Is my life really such an unheralded mess?
Or, is this path of distraught paths really the
god's way of kissing me, saying, "son, you are
indeed blessed."
These pills cloud me, the gods of medicine hear
my plea and require a copay, a fee.
My vowels propel through space and time,
With a rhyme I dance with the
art angels in a basement of grime.
Carry me on the wings of pestilence,
I refuse to let go of this golden glow.
4am 5am 6am

I wonder
where this absent cavity in my chest
will be filled.
I go to the ocean, to the sea,
only to see the waves lap against me and,
for a moment I feel free, yet still absent from life.
I traverse the plains to find myself
lost in an empty great wild American prairie expanse,
until I find myself trembling at the foothills

DEAR BOBBY

of the great mountains rocky of the west.
Climb, I must, or die alone and
hungry still absentness beating
within my chest.
4am 5am 6am

THE BUDDHA OF THIS SMALL TOWN

So many theories, so many distractions,
How can I get inside?
How the hell do I,
Being of my particular physiology, psychology and
Of a compartmentalized mind,
Which streams thought.
That lives in a darkened hollow of a head.
How do I become,
The Buddha, of this little town?
Who do I tell my tales to,
In the memory, like the hourglass and sand
Who do I love when I know what
Breaches the brain through the blood
In my veins, flowing through my body
And through this vessel I interpret life.
Questions keep me *alive*.
In separation lies the disorder.
Only harmony can equalize.
Who am I?
Who are you?
Bye.

Commercialized Punk and Traditional Religion

Going to the Philly Punk Rock Flee Market Holiday Extravaganza in December/
Going to 10th Presbyterian Church prior, 9'oclock service, 17th and Spruce/
To worship our Lord and savior Jesus Christ/
At the market I purchase the "Something in the Way" Nirvana single
Paired with The Misfits' "Lucifer's Penis Rising" single
Kurt R.I.P. we miss you
Danzig never fit in
At Church we prepare our hearts,
for devotion,
love is an ocean.
Better is one day in your arms than thousands elsewhere.

Pierre Auguste Renoir Puts On a Fresh Pot And Smokes A Cig

Putting on a fresh pot,
awaiting patiently, creatives:
a sorry emotional lot.
When will my Columbian elixir
fix my sluggardly despair!?
I ponder you, oh gods of
the coffee bean, enticing me to feel
serene, as I wander
through this, at times dreary dream.
Oh, mornings, you shall be
the death of me. A cigarette lit in the
darkness. Two coal embers burning
in this misty malcontent. Tis that
season. The season of my malcontent
has long since passed, unaided, by the Hamlet
of my dreams.

NOAH AND THE WHALE

Like two atoms in a molecule
we revolve around each other
until, an intruding, separate,
larger molecule, with more
Protons, more Electrons,
comes and steals our bond.
Now I am left with nothing but isotopes.

Dysfunctional Family

I know the feeling which reveals itself at night.
Believe me, I have been, I am, where you are;
My brothers
My sisters
I know this temptation that travels to you,
No matter how far you run,
Regardless where you remain.
I know the power of this...this...Demon.
Your dreams are mine,
Your struggles are the same,
My brothers
My sisters
I know the feeling which comes alive
In the morning, Prior to raising your
head from your pillow,
the feeling greets you with a sardonic
smile and living laugh, "You are mine,"
The demon steals your serene, He screeches.
My sisters
My brothers
Yet, he is wrong, nothing could be further
From the truth. YOU hold the power!
My brothers and sisters
I am here to hold you when the demons
come alive at night
at midday
at sunrise
I know the dream that comes alive at night.
I have met this demon which reveals himself,
this Prince of darkness, He can be
DEFEATED.

THE UNEXPLAINED LAW

Academic actualizations

Basic casualization

Compound connections

I am orbiting you

Blazing comet

Sultry satellite

Cold, convoluted

Sad

At my Aphelion

Warm and safe

At my closest approach to you

Blazing sun

Perihelion

Kepler couldn't keep

Us from colliding.

Another day in the books and I'm alive

Another day down and still I yet rise

Another day to look forward with the surprise of thriving

It's 4 am and the day is in the books

This book of days,

We know when it begins

But no one

When it ends

I smoke, drink malta, and end my day,

Another one for this book. I am the

hero, protagonist, villain antagonist, and all supporting rolls in between

The books they say, I say a day

Another day down

Down for the stage, This one

One's passions

A man

Must obey

For in mere hours

it will be as it always has

been and forever shall be

Another day.

Moving Mountains

Get free/
Be brave/
Surround yourself in light/
Pour love on everything/
The day will come when you're no longer fake
And the day comes when you no longer feel
Then the day comes when you'll no longer fear

Right to doubt

Will to doubt Bertrand Russell
VS.
WILL TO BELIEVE

We ever long for visions of beauty,
We ever dream of unknown worlds.
Computers and psychotherapists
Tell us our problems, our secret desires.
But they are merely metal, plastic, the same material of you and I.
How can machine or man quantify my emotions
I say, made by man, conquered by man, controlled by man, destroyed by man.
The will to doubt
VS
The will to believe

Is the ultimate conundrum of him, man, himself.
Man wants to believe.
This man screams off Brooklyn rooftops that he craves to believe.

IN RESPONSE TO A PORTRAIT

Like the portrait by John Singer Sargent,
of two helplessly hopelessly wedded souls.
The portrait was dim, even in 1897.
The couple grimly seeking searching reaching towards heaven,
timeless romantic.
Mr. and Mrs. Isaac Newton Phelps, who are you?
Starring through a century of fading oils, all my emotions become,
revoked. I sit and stare in repose.
What's left but to stoke the flame; the burning desire, love, and addiction.
Mr. Sargent did you understand my affliction?
Lest I travel back to the Rocky Mountains, those billowing rocks so beautifully captured
by your contemporaries, by Albert Bierstadt.
I am a lost wandering critic, traveling through time using paint as my medium, to form
these rhymes.
Ridding myself of a life that has become full of all things labeled tedium.
From the French to the Austrian to the English to the American, a new world unfurls.
All cultures aiming to capture the intrinsically fleeting moments of life, nature, and the
beautiful, as they curl.
In and out, a dance of colors, a pageantry of light yet again is unfurled.
Only then does my soul feel full and bright.
The fog clears as my headlights part the mist, and I realize, as these masters before me,
I do have
something to offer...
Love!
Forgiveness!
Hope!

...for a new tomorrow...
A new heaven.
A new Earth.
Today

Side by Side

just keep on walking
side by side
headlights streaming by in diminution
keep on walking by side by side
What a waste
chasing dreams away
at times a tacky phrase
is all that someone can say,
ever say.
Sometimes, the lost days are golden,
often times, they are just pools set apart-
isolated collection of loose bonds
chemical streams swirl,
littering the consciousness,
the collective consciousness
Split slide multiply and die
back & forth
our legs move ahead
side by side we move our hearts
what is it all worth to you?
ask yourself.
Before you just keep on walking and wandering on
But, *always*, no matter what, keep on keep on walking by child.

Seahorse Corpses in my Drawer

Harness the evil

Stamp out Your demons

Send the swine hurtling off the cliffs of forever

A mad king sits atop a crown of broken glass

A dead pop princess screams me to sleep

For forever and a day the prodigals

are always running away

My brother is my keeper

in keeping me insane

Go down to the railroad

You will see the past present and future

Roll into the distance like a faded man's dreams

An expired whisper escapes into the stale air

as daggers cut me to sleep

Lusting for nature's delights
A glance to the heavens
From the floor of the forest
Reveals a distant star
Symbolizing neither near or far
A twinkling image destroys the ego
Although in this here woodland
Anything goes
I am the king
No fiction
But here, take this benediction
First came confliction
Then came conviction
Wasn't careful took a stumble into addiction
What happens next is anyone's guess
The truth only goes as far as the rocks thrown
So I asked the reapers which way to go
Take a trip beside me along memory lane
My past has no real pain
And no thank you I would not like any fame
I really have nothing to gain but catharsis
So please, don't call me an artist.
Please call me the man who could not deal with the beauty and treachery of life so
he wrote after lusting for nature's delights.

The Planes of Sedonia

That face
Looking down at our suspended spinning blue crystal
Shouts a link through time blazoned from the eye of RA
Staring back out into that Martian space
Man's roots are in the stars

Don't give in no matter how appetizing
The Dark Bids get
If one must be a slave to fate
Let the gods hear your cries of dissonance
No retreat
Revolt!

Leave demons behind an iron door
Deadbolt!
Leave distractions confined, tied down on the floor
Release
without drowning in the tumult!

Shimmering Isles of oblivion
Lost in transparent trappings of a silver soldier
Whichever way the wind blows
That's where my dreams escape me

VESSELS

I pour myself into you
Who, as an empty basin,
Allowed me to fill you up to the brim,
But kept me from ever overflowing.
I pour myself into you
Who, as an elegant, yet twisted and cracking vase,
Forced me into the confines of your contours,
Eventually I come dripping out the top, and through the cracks.
I pour myself into you
Who, as three separate bowls,
hold me safely, but compartmentalized from myself,
I long to be whole again.
I poured myself out
Onto the withered crippled decayed concrete,
Only to wash away at the slightest rain,
away with the refuse
Down Dead Man's alley.
I poured myself out
Into my own trembling hands,
Breathlessly hoping to hold my sanity together in outstretched arms to heaven,
Palms cupped trying to cradle myself together,
But with every bump and misstep I lose a drop of myself to the open air,
Ending with brittle dry hands holding no moisture.
I poured myself out
And down my own arrogant throat,
pleasantly drunk on myself, "Cheers! to fucking me,"
Until I vomit and am up and down the drain.
I pour myself into
My Father's fertile soil,
and sit back patiently for harvest.

I cultivate my land, this is my Garden,
mumblings of Voltaire and l'optimisme,
I watch my flowers bud.

I poured myself out and into you,
but I am still here,
yet here I still stand.

She Says

I don't sleep very well anymore
Well, I never slept well
Except now this ceiling fan
Keeps me up all night
But there is no ceiling fan
It's just you
In my mind
Going around and around and around

An icicle hangs in the sun

So serene

So in the moment, Awareness is subjective

In its own way of vanishing,

It goes back to the cycle, which will

One day, bring her back to me, as an icicle

Trapped in the cycle, melting in the sun.

Consciousness is subjective

A blade of grass

Poking through the dirt reaching up to the sun

An organic skyscraper to some

Awaits my blade

Is pain subjective?

I'm just trying to see the world through the world's own eyes.

What would this world see through my eyes?

Would it look into the mirror or look into the sky?

LOWER LETTER EYE

i tasted death's kiss salty yet sweet
i kissed death then spit in his face
death i betray you thus,
go with the Romans needn't make a fuss
i crucify you while laughing at the absurdity
for i know you shall rise again
and i will dance with you once more
allow you to take me home and tuck me in
just not today, not today
i still have some fight left
my future from me you will not cleft

be gone from my sights i never knew you
on your lips i will only chew
you are thirsty for me, i know
sponge soaked in vinegar i carry in tow
i will crucify you again, stand tall and bellow,
"I AM SAVED BY JESUS."